The Politics of Faith

THE POLITICS OF FAITH
The Bible, Government, and Public Policy

Jerry L. Sumney

FORTRESS PRESS

MINNEAPOLIS

THE POLITICS OF FAITH

The Bible, Government, and Public Policy

Print ISBN: 978-1-5064-6699-6

eBook ISBN: 978-1-5064-6700-9

Cover design: Lindsey Owens

Cover images: Building Vectors / GreenTana / iStockphoto

For Kenneth Mick

*a minister and friend who seeks
to hear God's word for our world*

Contents

Preface   *ix*

1. Introduction: Is It That Bad or Is It Politics As Usual?   *1*

2. The Witness of the Mosaic Covenant   *11*

3. The Witness of the Prophets   *23*

4. Acts: The Earliest Church and Economic Systems   *33*

5. Matthew's Jesus on the Church's Mission   *43*

6. Expectations for Nations in Parables of Jesus   *53*

7. Luke and Care for Those Who Are Poor and Disadvantaged   *65*

8. Paul, the Ruler of This World, and Sin (with a Capital S)   *77*

9. The Example of Jesus and the Good of Others   *93*

10. Revelation on World Governments   *103*

11. Being a Faithful Church in Today's World   *115*

Notes   *133*

Preface

This book is a call for the church to use its voice to speak about political and social issues. I think that too many within the church remain silent as policies are instituted and laws are enacted that run contrary to what Scripture points to as God's will. This book will have served its purpose if it enables readers to give biblical reasons for taking stands for some laws and policies, and against others. As I will argue, the Bible has much to say about what governments should be concerned about. It further expects God's people to work to bring as much of the world as possible, including political institutions, into conformity with God's will. Some voices from particular branches of the church have been so narrowly focused that they have supported many things that violate God's will, or have supported a few things, or perhaps one thing, they think is most important. I hope to show that God is concerned about a broad range of issues. I believe that listening to the Bible requires us to stand against some cultural ideals that have been made into law and policy and in some cases seem to have been baptized into the church. I hope that a fresh look at the biblical texts can help us see God's will more clearly and enable us to say why we think it is God's will. This book grew out of a Lay School of Theology class at Lexington Theological Seminary. The thoughts and questions of those who have attended that program over the years have often moved me to think more clearly and carefully about the implications of the topics we have studied. I also want to thank Scott Tunseth and Carla Barnhill at Fortress Press for their careful reading and good suggestions about this book.

1

Introduction: Is It That Bad or Is It Politics As Usual?

The nations are in an uproar, the kingdoms totter . . .
The Lord of hosts is with us; the God of Jacob is our refuge.
—Psalm 46:8

We seem to be in a time of great tension and turmoil. Language and behavior seem to have become more crude and more rude. Greed is celebrated and immorality is seen as inconsequential. Our political leaders encourage us to fear one another, and our churches are supporting policies that harm people who are vulnerable. Many of us are shocked that things have gotten to the point where it is considered acceptable for a national leader to denigrate publicly a former rival after that rival has died. I agree with those who say that the political and cultural environment is poison, is unchristian.

But our current situation may not be as surprising as we believe it to be. Just thinking back over the last sixty years of the twentieth century provides too many examples of racial and social injustice and discrimination, often blessed or perpetuated by much of the church. During World War II, our government adopted a racist policy that took property from and interned citizens of Japanese descent. We feared and distrusted these people just because their ancestors were from Japan. Then Joe McCarthy terrorized and ruined the careers of people who wouldn't conform to his political outlook. Or think of the tensions of the '60s, when racial injustice and social inequities provoked riots that torched neighborhoods. There was unrest on college campuses that included violence and the destruction of property. At the same time, African Americans were being beaten in the streets by the police because they were trying to have their rights recognized. And how can we forget the Nixon years, when a president ordered people to commit crimes for political gain and then lied about it? Unfortunately, the church was on record supporting internment, McCarthy, Nixon, and even those who beat protesters.

Few decades have passed without having some kind of evil being invigorated and gaining ground in the United States. But we thought we had moved forward as a society. We have been thinking that we are beyond some ways of thinking and of behaving toward one another. It's not that we thought we had conquered all social evils, but we thought that at least we would never slide back into some habits and outlooks of earlier decades. We were sure that our social and cultural norms had moved forward so much that those problems of the twentieth century could no longer haunt us. But it seems we have not made as much progress as we thought.

We know that lying is not new to public officials. But the number and volume and brazenness of the lies flowing out of our news feeds and from our politicians seem unusual, even if not new. There seems to be a renewed willingness to be open with our rudeness, especially on social media, and to allow tacit acceptance of social ills that we thought were being overcome or were at least unacceptable in the public sphere. But racism again can be given the thin veil of national security, and so be accepted. It is with good reason that we feel uncomfortable, even sullied, by the way things are.

Christians in mainline churches seem to be the ones who feel most strongly and broadly that things have gone terribly wrong. Throughout much of the twentieth century, mainline churches identified themselves with the values of the dominant culture. This identification with the culture did not mean that the church was unable to critique certain aspects of it. It seemed that the church was managing to shape the culture in some ways but, at the same time, the culture was shaping the church. This connection helped both the church and some elements of society and the government work against structures that supported racism and sexism, as some of these churches worked for desegregation and fuller rights for women. But it also meant that the church accepted and adopted unjust social structures and tacitly supported an economic system that increasingly advantaged people who were wealthier. Members of these churches were among those who gained advantages, and so the churches themselves profited from those systems.

Meanwhile, another branch of the church was feeling more and more alienated in the last half of the twentieth century. Evangelicals felt that their understanding of the faith and of the nation was under attack. They saw a moral decay in the nation as there were changes in cultural standards in the arena of personal morality. They felt that their voices were not being heeded by those in power as they saw the nation rejecting values they believed to be God's will. The changes that mainline churches worked for sometimes seemed to have harmful consequences for some members of evangelical churches. Calls for equality felt like threats to some members' jobs, and governmental social programs challenged the value they placed on individual freedom and responsibility.

Some within the evangelical community seem to think that the focus of politicians and pundits is returning to things they think are important. Some, but not all, are willing to turn a blind eye to support policies that make some social ills worse if they can see gains in areas that seem to support of their beliefs about personal morality. Some refuse to see racism in our national immigration debates and policies, perhaps in part because they see movement toward banning abortion or returning Christian prayer to events at public schools.

Part of the differences between mainline and evangelical churches about political stances and issues seems to come from the difference in the sphere of ethics each emphasizes. Mainline churches focus on social issues and are reluctant to make demands about personal morality. That is, they are interested in eradicating racism or protecting the environment but don't want to talk about personal sexual ethics. (This is where our individualistic cultural outlook shows itself in these churches.) On the other hand, evangelicals seem to focus on personal morality, including personal sexual conduct, and overt expressions of their faith, while they seem less interested in changing unjust social structures that support long-standing social ills, such as racism and persistent poverty. While these generalizations do not fit all members of these groups, they seem to capture significant majorities of them. Among the exceptions are the Black churches, which often speak of both personal and social morality.

So, what kinds of things should the church be concerned about, and what should it do about them? In this book, we will think about some of the kinds of policy questions the church should speak about. We will think about what the Bible indicates that God wants for the world and how that comes to expression in public and political life. It is not enough for the church to adopt or reject cultural liberalism or cultural conservatism. If we want to act as the church, we need biblical and theological reasons for adopting our positions on questions of social and personal morality. If the church is going to act as the people of God, it must ground its action in explicitly Christian reasons. This book will focus on questions of social morality while recognizing the importance of personal morality for the Christian life.

As we ask religious/theological questions, we must also think about the church's role in influencing the development of policies and laws. For nearly everyone, it is not really a question of whether the church should influence our laws—it is only a question of which issues we speak on. Some who might say the church has no business working for laws that limit the power of employers might well say that the church should work to stop gay marriage or limits on Christian prayer in public schools. Then, some who say the church should work for laws that give advantages to people in poverty might well say that the church should stay out of laws that govern whom a person can marry. When we affirm that there needs to be a separation of church and state, we don't really mean that the church should have no influence. That is certainly not what that political doctrine has meant historically. Christian beliefs have always influenced how we vote and the laws we live by.

Ideas about the church's role in shaping government policies and programs vary widely. When it comes to dealing with the plight of those who are experiencing poverty and issues of unemployment, for example, Richard Chewing summarized the consensus of evangelical scholars by ranking those responsible for helping the economically disadvantaged. The list from most responsible to least goes: The poor person himself or herself, friends and family, church and nongovernment agencies, owners of businesses, and last, the government.[1] D. C. Innes says explicitly that limited government is the biblical form of government. He bases this on his reading of 1 Peter 2:13–15 and Romans 13, in which he asserts that the government is seen to have the power to punish evil, but is not charged to do good.[2]

I believe that these understandings of the Bible and the place of the church in shaping the government and its policies seriously misrepresent what is actually in the Bible. The list above of those responsible for helping people who are poor seems to owe more to a culture of individualism than to the biblical witness. And citing what is *not* talked about in a couple of texts is hardly a good biblical foundation for the assertion that governments should not do good. In the chapters that follow, we will look at how different parts of the Bible envision the relationship between the will of God and the political, social, and economic systems of their time. I want us to think about the question of the place of the church in these discussions through the theological lens of the biblical texts. We will look at how various biblical writers see the place of the people of God and the will of God in discussions of social and economic issues. As we go through various parts of the Bible, we will see what kinds of things God has called God's people to be involved in and how God calls them to shape the world they live in. It is my hope that we can use these biblical examples to help us talk about the church's role in discussions of social policies and what kinds of positions the Bible calls it to take on them.

This is a book written to help readers think about how faith can and should shape what we think about the ways our culture and government deal with a wide range of issues, including those that relate to the economic and social policies of our governments. I also want us to think about our policies and laws as they affect people of different social and economic classes. This book provides reasons for the church to be involved in shaping our laws and culture to be more just and merciful. It helps us talk about these issues through what we find in the Bible. I believe there are good Christian reasons to advocate for policies that privilege the good of people who are poor and vulnerable. And I think there are good Christian reasons to say that attempts to maintain the status quo or favor those who are wealthy (including supposed "job creators") violate the will of God. As we go through the biblical texts, we will see that the people of God as a group and the nations and cultures to which they belong have obligations to the disadvantaged and needy people among them. What we see will challenge our individualistic cultural outlook.

In many places, the parts of the church that have favored policies and laws that promote more just economic and social systems have been unwilling to speak as Christians about those commitments. Too often we have felt that those who focus on the individual and the individual's salvation can speak from Scripture in ways we cannot. I want this book to give a solid biblical foundation to the church's work for more just social and economic policies. I hope that it enables readers to have conversations about the kinds of policies God's people should support based on what we find in Scripture. What we see in the Bible can help us make the case for saying that policies that help people who are econically and socially vulnerable and require the well-off to contribute to the common good bring us closer to what God expects of nations. I hope it empowers churches and individual readers to be able to challenge Christians who oppose such policy directions, and even convince them to join the fight for a more just world. As we will see, the weight of the biblical witness calls for more just and merciful social and economic systems.

I believe this biblical foundation will help us approach moving our laws and policies toward the will of God as Christians, as people who engage in this work because it is God's will. It is a part of our witness to the world. This does not mean that we do not welcome non-Christians who want to work toward the same goals. But we need biblical reasons to support our view when we talk with fellow Christians. Many of those Christian reasons are also widely accepted humanitarian reasons. Since we share those values with non-Christians, they also can be a solid basis for working with non-Christians for common goals.

Questions for Discussion

1. What is your experience of political discourse in the present moment? What effect does remembering the past episodes and acts mentioned at the beginning of this chapter have on your evaluation of the present?

2. Have the churches you have experienced (both congregations and denominations) been more willing to talk about social sins (e.g., racism) or personal sin (e.g., sexual ethics)? Why do you think that is the case?

3. Do you think the Bible should influence what Christians think about political, social, and economic issues? Why or why not?

4. Do you think the Bible should influence what Christians think about personal ethics? Why or why not?

5. If you answered questions 3 and 4 differently, why? If you had the same answer for both, why?

6. Do you feel reluctant to talk about political, social, and economic issues with others? With Christians? Why or why not?

2

The Witness of the Mosaic Covenant

You shall not pervert the justice due to your poor.
—Exodus 23:6

In this chapter, we will begin to look at how the Hebrew Bible (the Christian Old Testament), especially books of the Law, views the relationship between faithful living and the social and economic systems of Israel's government and the governments of the other nations they come in contact with. While the relationship between the church and the government in western democracies is different from that between the state and the religious, social, and political institutions of Israel, we can still see the ways that God's will influenced the way they organized their social systems.

When we think about the Covenant (Law) of Moses, we usually think of it as a religious system. It has the Ten Commandments, the temple system, the purity laws, and other rules about how to worship God. But the Law is not just about religious matters. Even the Ten Commandments have laws about theft and murder, matters that civil authorities deal with. The Law of the Hebrew Bible sets out a way of organizing families and the whole of society. It has regulations about banking, interest rates (Exod 22:25–27), the treatment of animals (Exod 23:5, 12; Deut 25:4), the justice system (Exod 23:1–3), and a system for providing for people who are poor (Lev 23:22) that includes a debt relief system (Lev 25). It has environmental laws (Lev 25 calls for sabbatical years for farm fields) and laws about how to treat immigrants and foreigners (Exod 22:21–24).

Part of the way the Israelites are to live as the people of God is to keep the Ten Commandments that appear in Exodus 20:1–17. Yet what follows is as much a part of the covenant as the Ten Commandments themselves. These chapters set out laws about the social and economic systems and about personal morality. The next few verses of chapter 20 tell of the people's reaction to receiving the covenant (vv. 18–21), then move on to instructions about how to build an altar to worship God (vv. 22–26). Chapter 21 starts with God saying to Moses, "These are the ordinances you shall set before them." The first laws listed here are about how to treat people who were enslaved. The Hebrew people could not envision not having slaves, but these laws require kinds of protections that the law codes of the Israelites' neighbors did not have, laws that recognized the humanity of enslaved people. In addition, chapters 21–23 have laws about the legal responses to violent acts, about land and livestock ownership and treatment, about the punishment of thieves and the restoration of stolen property, and about sexual behavior.

Exodus does not distinguish between religious laws and economic laws and social policies. In Exodus 22:20, we see a command not to worship any other gods. In the very next verses (vv. 21–24), we find this law about how to treat immigrants and other vulnerable members of society:

> Whoever sacrifices to any god, other than the Lord alone, shall be devoted to destruction. You shall not wrong or oppress a resident alien, for you were aliens in the land of Egypt. You shall not abuse any widow or orphan. If you do abuse them, when they cry out to me, I will surely heed their cry; my wrath will burn, and I will kill you with the sword, and your wives shall become widows and your children orphans.

It is as much a religious obligation to be sure that immigrants are treated justly as it is to worship only God. This is especially striking because in most places at the time, immigrants were basically without rights. People had protections within social units or nations because of their connections to others within the system. Displaced people lived without these protections. But God demands that immigrants receive justice, reminding the Israelites that they know what it is like to be strangers without rights.

Widows and orphans are mentioned here as other vulnerable people within society. Like immigrants, they were without the usual connections and without many economic possibilities. So, they were to be protected. It seems to make God particularly upset when these sorts of people are treated unjustly. If we keep reading chapter 22, we see that the next law is about banking practices:

> If you lend money to my people, to the poor among you, you shall not deal with them as a creditor; you shall not exact interest from them. If you take your neighbor's cloak in pawn, you shall restore it before the sun goes down; for it may be your neighbor's only clothing to use as cover; in what else shall

that person sleep? And if your neighbor cries out to me, I will listen, for I am compassionate. (vv. 25–27)

This law protects poor people from being overcharged with interest; in fact, it prohibits those who are wealthy from charging people who are poor any interest at all. Neither can the banker keep the poor person's collateral given to secure the loan. While there were significant penalties for not repaying a debt, the protections in this text are given so that repayment is more likely possible and there is no additional burden on the people least able to bear it. It is not the profits of the "job creators" that are protected, but rather the needy child of the creator of all things. We should note that this law does not prohibit charging interest. It only prohibits charging interest to *poor people*. There can be no payday lenders for those in covenant with God.

This law protecting people who are poor is immediately followed by the command, "You shall not revile God" (v. 28). Again, we see that God is as interested in economic policy as in proper worship. After a few more laws that have to do with worship practices, Exodus returns to civil policy, with a focus on legal proceedings. The final command in this set is, "You shall not oppress a resident alien; you know the heart of an alien, for you were aliens in the land of Egypt" (23:9). The repetition of these commands about immigrants helps us see both how unusual such laws were (they had to be named repeatedly) and how important they were as part of the covenant with God.

Again, these commands immediately follow the Ten Commandments. This is a clear indication that God's covenant is about more than religious regulations; it is about building the kind of society that will reflect what God wants and even who God is. We see that God is concerned about personal and social morality. God is as concerned about the structures of the economic and social systems as God is concerned about sexual behavior and dietary restrictions. God is concerned with both, and both are mixed into commands about proper worship. They are a package deal.

The shape of these commands takes on even fuller significance when we think about the composition of Exodus. While the headings in some Bibles say that the first five books (the Pentateuch) were written by Moses, there are good reasons for thinking they are not—including that the death and burial of Moses are recorded in them. The stories and traditions contained in Exodus and the other books of the Pentateuch go back as far as the tenth century B.C.E., but they were not written as we have them until the time of the Babylonian exile after the fall of Jerusalem in 587 B.C.E. Following that defeat, all the Israelites of any intellectual, political, or religious significance were forced to live in Babylon (today's Iraq) to keep them from fomenting any more revolts against the Babylonian Empire. It is while the people were displaced, without their own government and not allowed to live in their homeland, that they put together the books of the Pentateuch (also called the Torah).

These books are an amazing expression of faith. The authors and editors wrote them not just as a guide for how to live in exile, but also as a blueprint for how to construct the kind of society God wants when they returned to their homeland. This means they were trusting in God to remain in covenant with them even though they had been so unfaithful that God had finally given them over to the Babylonians. They understood the exile to be the result of their failure to live as they should in the covenant rather than being a sign that God was too weak to save them. They were also confident that their powerful God would not forsake them. As unfaithful as they had been, God continued to be in a covenant relationship with them. The exile is what they should have expected, given their behavior. It is what the terms of the covenant called for. Once in Babylon, they affirmed that God loves them and remained in that relationship with them. This meant that God would return them to the land of their ancestors. The laws they set out in Exodus were to help them live the faithful life in a way they had never done before. They set out the way God wanted them to live when they returned.

Given that these books were written when there was no Israelite government (and this is true even if Moses wrote them), they set out what the writers thought should happen rather than what they believed they could get a king or a clan leader to agree to. It is in that context that they set out these economic and social protections for people who are vulnerable, immigrants, and even the land itself. Their vision was limited by their time and social setting, and so they kept some systems that we now understand to be completely unjust (e.g., slavery). But even in those cases, they often prohibited the ways those systems had allowed people to be mistreated. When they wrote, they were the migrants. They were the people without the full protections that Babylonian citizens had. They knew the injustice they endured and were confident that this was not how God wants humans to be treated.

But experiences of injustice were not the only or the primary motivators of their plan for how to organize society. The biblical writers sometimes gave a theological foundation for these instructions about how to live as God's people. That is, they said, "Here is the religious reason for this law." We have already read some reasons. They were to treat immigrants justly because they were immigrants themselves and so knew the damage injustice does to immigrants. But more often the reason rests in who God is. The laws reflect the character of God. We can see this clearly in Leviticus.

Levitical Laws

Leviticus is an amazing book. It may not be scintillating reading for us, but it is a work of enormous faith. This book has lots of instructions about how to behave in the temple, how to offer various sacrifices, schedules for holy days, descriptions of clothes priests are to wear, and all kinds of other details about religious life. What makes this amazing is that the book was written when there was no temple. The Babylonians had torn down the Jerusalem temple, but the priests who wrote Leviticus trusted God so much that they had complete confidence that there would again be a temple for God. They wanted their descendants to be ready to run the temple in just the way God wants, so they preserved all of these instructions for posterity.

But the writers of Leviticus also knew that God would not accept their worship if the people lived in ways that violated the covenant. So, Leviticus also contains instructions on how to organize the Israelites' social and economic systems. Leviticus 17:1–26:46 is often referred to as the "Holiness Code." After the first sixteen chapters of Leviticus, which cover the rules for conducting temple worship, the Holiness Code tells the people how to live lives that are holy. Living in these ways was necessary to make their worship acceptable. The writers regularly tell the people to "be holy," which has two meanings here: to be separate and to be morally upright. God's people are to be different, separate from their neighbors so that they stand apart as the people who worship only God. Their moral lives are a part of that.

The people are to be holy in both of those senses because God is holy in both of those senses. God is different from all other beings, so Israel is to be different from all other nations. And God is morally upright, so the Israelites are to be morally upright. The Holiness Code says this explicitly in many places. The authors give voice to God, who speaks directly, saying, "You shall be holy, for I the Lord your God am holy" (19:2; 20:7, 26; 21:6, 8). This general command sometimes introduces a set of some specific commands that deal with expectations about worship practices and other specifically religious duties. Other times it supports sets of commands about social and economic practices. Sometimes this grounding is incorporated into the list of commands and sometimes it follows a list, clearly supporting the whole group.

In addition to the places where this phrase supports commands, there are numerous places that use a short-hand for it that connects commands to the character of God. In 18:4, God speaking to Moses says, "My ordinances you shall observe and my statutes you shall keep, following them: I am the Lord your God." God says the people are to keep the commands because of who God is. This "I am the Lord your God" appears in 18:4, 30; 19:3, 4, 10, 25, 31, 34; 20:7; 23:22, 43; 24:22; 25:17, 55; and 26:1. Its repetition means that it is important for the lives of God's people to reflect the character of God. Their conduct is to show people who God is. As we have noted, these commands were not just about personal morality and private religious practices. As Leviticus sets it out, the Israelites are to make their economic and social systems conform to the character of God. Those systems are to be just because God is just. Those systems are to show mercy to those who need mercy because God is merciful. Their systems are to promote holy living because God is holy. As we noted above, Exodus 22:27 says creditors must return the collateral of poor people because, God says, "I am compassionate." It is not just that God is pleased by justice, mercy, holiness, and compassion. God *is* these things. All aspects of the lives of God's people are to exemplify all of these aspects of God's character. That is, their lives are to show the world who God is.

We have seen that the covenant God makes with Israel includes instructions about religious behavior, personal morality, and social and economic morality. We have also seen that these instructions are based on who God is. The expectation of these books of the Bible is that the people of God will mirror the character of God in their conduct in all of their personal and corporate lives. Reflecting God in civic life means taking care of and giving special protections to people who are vulnerable. Among those protected are orphans, widows, immigrants, and broadly people who are poor. The social and economic systems are to protect them because protecting them is the way God's people live out and embody the God who protects people who are in vulnerable positions and graciously gives all things.

What Does the Law Say to the Church Today?

So, what do these instructions in the Law suggest about what the church should be concerned about and about how the church should go about expressing that concern? Some would argue that the Law says little to the church today because we do not live in a government ruled by God or the religious authorities. Of course, it is right to note that the Israelites, at least part of the time, talked about God being their king. But they also had a human king on the throne and civic laws that demanded obedience. Some might also note that Christians are not bound to the Mosaic covenant. This is also true, but it does not mean that we are not to learn from the Law. In fact, the Apostle Paul says we are to learn how to live from what we read in these books (1 Cor 9:11). We even find 1 Peter 1:15–16 supporting its commands with: "You shall be holy because I am holy." The commandments we have examined here show us what it meant to reflect God's holiness in the time these books were written. They show us that social and economic laws and policies that reflect who God is are those that provide special protections, even advantages, to people who are in vulnerable positions and that these protections are to be paid for by the wealthy.

Some might argue that the church should be responsible for the people who are vulnerable rather than the government. But Israel's laws show how problematic that view is. Note that these commands do not tell the temple to help those who are disadvantaged in and by the social and economic systems of the time. The job of caring for and protecting vulnerable people is not just the job of religious institutions. The commands call God's people to construct economic and social systems and laws that reflect God's holiness, justice, love, and compassion. They do not allow God's people to compartmentalize their lives so that they care for people who are poor at church but take no account of them when formulating the laws that govern social and economic policy.

The character of God remains the standard for how God expects God's people to live. Christians do not need to be in the Mosaic covenant to have God's character be the guide for all aspects of their lives. We have already noted that

1 Peter quotes Leviticus's call to make God's holiness the guide for the Christian's conduct. The book of Ephesians makes the same point by calling the church to "be imitators of God" (Eph 5:1). If we take the Word of God as we hear it in the Law seriously, the church will work for social and economic systems that protect, and even give advantages to, people who are in vulnerable positions.

Questions for Discussion

1. How might the command about not charging interest to poor people in Exodus influence the ways banks today structure loans? What would this command suggest about today's common practice of charging lower interest rates to people who have the means to borrow more money? What stand might the church take about such practices?

2. What does the command about not charging poor people interest suggest about payday loan companies? How might the church speak out about such practices? What role might the church play in shaping laws about such practices?

3. What do the commands in Exodus about treating strangers and foreigners suggest about our immigration policies? What might it look like to have an immigration policy that provided justice and protections from mistreatment?

4. What kinds of systems do we have that give advantages to wealthy people? What do the things we have read about in the Law suggest about what the church should say about such systems? What is the church's role in trying to shape them?

5. What do you think about the idea that Christians are to be holy because they are the people of a God who is holy? How might that holiness be lived in ways that go beyond personal morality?

6. The Law tells Israel how to organize its legal, economic, and social systems. What does that say about how the church should relate to shaping those systems in our context?

3

The Witness of the Prophets

Listen, you heads of Jacob and rulers of the house of Israel!
Should you not know justice?

—Micah 3:1

Those who call on the church to be involved with social issues often draw heavily on the prophets, and with good reason. We will look briefly at some of the most-cited passages, but I want us to pay attention to the prophets' primary audiences. Taking note of this along with their messages can help us think further about whether or how the church should participate in discussions of social and economic policy today.

We tend to think of prophets as pastors who address primarily the religious community, the gathering of the faithful. While prophets would have done much of this, their primary audience, at least in the writings they have left behind, was often the political leaders of their day. In the stories of the Israelites coming into and settling in Canaan, for example, the function of the prophet seems to be performed by military leaders. God regularly talks to Joshua, telling him how to proceed and even telling him when people have done wrong. Joshua even leads the people in renewing the covenant with God (Josh 8:30–35). As the military and political leader of the Israelites, he famously ends his career with what we would call a sermon, including calling the people to faithfulness to the covenant and to God (Josh 23–24).

The book of Judges tells of the time before the Israelites had a central government. The tribes seemed to be fairly independent, but they also maintained ties with one another. The stories that the book of Judges tells are about military leaders who rose when the Israelites' enemies had taken political control over parts of the land where the tribes lived. The book always attributes these difficulties to the people turning away from worshipping only God to worshipping other gods. When this happened, God called a leader to bring the tribes together to form an army that regained the territory. (The Samson story is an exception to this pattern.) As these military leaders arose, they also became religious leaders who often called the people to be faithful to God.

Think about where these leaders had to come from before God called them. They had to be people with significant status in the community. If they were not from among the recognizably powerful class, they would not be able to convince the leaders of the tribes to join their cause. The story doesn't always tell us about the social position of the leader, but when it does, the person is well placed. Deborah was already known as a prophet and already served as a person who adjudicated civil cases in her district (4:4–5).

Gideon was from the family that was in charge of Baal worship for his region and so was influential (6:19–35). And Jephthah had such a reputation as a warrior that the leaders of the region of Gilead asked him to be their leader (11:1–11). What we can see from this is that the word of God comes to leaders, to those with status and power. It is the military and political leaders who call the people to faithfulness. The people that the word of God comes to are those who are in a position to shape the way the civil systems operate.

These judges don't function in the same way as the prophets will in the times that follow, but they show us a connection between God's calling the people to faithfulness and the political leadership of the Israelites. The book of 1 Samuel begins with an account of the decades just prior to the anointing of the first Israelite king, Saul. We learn about two powerful priests (Eli and Samuel) who also serve as prophets, as the ones who receive God's word for the people. These are the people who control the sanctuary where the Ark of the Covenant is kept. The presence of the Ark shows that this is a very important worship site. Eli's successor, Samuel, has such status that the tribes come to him when they want a king to be appointed. He is the one who eventually appoints Saul. The stories about Samuel set at least some of the pattern for Israelite prophets, including how they have access to the nation's leaders.

After Saul becomes king, Samuel remains a powerful priest. It is important to notice that he is a person with regular and easy access to the king. He comes to the king with both assurances and condemnations. When Saul has proven himself too unfaithful to God and to the instructions Samuel gives him from God, Samuel appoints Saul's successor. This successor is not in line to take the throne, and he is not even in Saul's family. Yet Samuel has the power to appoint David as the next king.

Speaking to Power

It is not just Samuel who has access to the king. Throughout the stories in 2 Samuel and 1 and 2 Kings, prophets continue to have easy access to the king. The prophet Nathan condemns David for his sins against Bathsheba and her husband Uriah. While it is clear that prophets have access to the king, we don't see much more about them until the nation is divided some sixty years later. Then they appear to have constant access to the kings. This indicates that the prophets have enough status and power that they are able to secure a meeting with the highest official in the country on a regular basis. In fact, when prophets appear in 1 and 2 Kings and 1 and 2 Chronicles, they are usually talking to kings or sometimes to other high-ranking government officials. The biggest exceptions are the stories about Elisha. He interacts with a number of people outside the royal circle, but even then it is often with people in power. He heals an army general of leprosy, and he is in a meeting with the local ruling council when the king of Israel sends an assassin to kill him (2 Kgs 6–7).

Prophets are people involved with governmental affairs. There are far more prophets than those named in the text and those who have books named after them. In 1 Kings 18:4, a man named Obadiah (not the prophet) saves 150 prophets from being killed. In several places there are references to what the NRSV calls "the company of the prophets" (e.g., 1 Sam 19:20; 1 Kgs 20:35). In 2 Kings 2, there is a "company of prophets" in Bethel and one in Jericho (2:3–5). A "company of prophets" seems to be something like the guild, which likely included the schooling needed to become and be recognized as a prophet. There seem to have been such groups in several cities, including Jerusalem. In Jerusalem, at least, they were on the payroll of the king. And not all the prophets on the payroll were prophets of the God of Israel. The story of Elijah having a contest with the prophets of Baal on Mt. Carmel says that 400 prophets of Baal were there. And they were all being paid by the king.

The prophets have such ready access to the king that he knows them by sight. This is true not only for prophets like Isaiah and Jeremiah, but also for some unnamed prophets (1 Kgs 20:41). Being known and paid by the king put some pressure on prophets to say what the king wanted to hear. The biblical texts often accuse the mass of prophets of prophesying falsely by saying what the king wants to hear (e.g., 1 Kgs 22:6–13; 2 Chron 18:5–12; Jer 5:31; Mic 3:5–6). Clearly, these prophets are not speaking primarily to the average person on the street. Their messages are spoken most directly to those in power, to the people who run the government.

We see the same thing when we look at the books of the prophets. Micah names the rulers as his audience in 3:1 and 9. Even when he calls all people to listen, he speaks of the sins of the capital cities of Israel and Judah (1:2–6). Similarly, Amos says that judgment is coming on Israel because of the unjust behavior of the rich (2:6–7; 5:10–12). And he makes it clear that the wealthy people are his target audience when he speaks of the "cows of Bashan" who live in luxury (4:1) and those who lie on ivory beds (6:4–6). His message of social justice is addressed to the rich who abuse the people who are poor. And as we see prophets do in the "historical books," Amos addresses the king (7:10–11).

Besides all the stories of Isaiah being in the king's presence, he sometimes says he is speaking to those who make the laws (Isa 10:1–4). The prophet Jeremiah is in either the king's presence or at the Jerusalem temple (which is sponsored by the king) all the time. Jeremiah even writes a long message to the king and sends his servant to get an audience with the king to read it to him (Jer 36).

All of this shows us that the messages of these prophets were directed to those in power. These messages were intended for the people who were in a position to shape social, economic, and judicial law. These kinds of people are the primary recipients of Micah's message about what God wants. The famous summary of Micah 6:6–9 says that God does not want the worship of people whose lives do not conform to the conduct that God demands. He says that no amount of extravagant worship can be acceptable if the worshipper does not do justice, love kindness (or mercy), and be humble before God. Acceptable worshippers must reflect the character of God, the justice and mercy of God, in their dealings with fellow humans. God demands this of all people, but Micah has made it clear that governmental authorities are a central focus. Micah's accusations in chapter 3 name the "rulers" as those who commit the injustices that are about to bring judgment (3:1, 9, 11). When the injustices that bring judgment are recited again in chapter 7, it is officials and judges who are mentioned as the perpetrators (7:2–4).

A Message to the Nations

We have seen that the Hebrew prophets addressed much of their message to the policymakers of the day. They clearly thought that the political, economic, and judicial systems of the nation should reflect the character of God. This is not the case just because the nation was a theocracy. It is not only the nations of the Israelites whom God expected to act justly and to have legal systems that reflected God's justice and mercy. The book of Amos begins with a series of accusations against the other nations of the region. Amos says God is bringing judgment on these nations because of their unjust conduct. He focuses on the extreme violence they commit in wars with one another (1:3, 11, 13; 2:1) and on their deceitful breaking of treaties (1:9, 11). Amos says that God has expectations for all nations.

The book of Jonah also shows clearly that God has expectations for all nations. The prophet Jonah is sent to Nineveh, the capital of what the original readers saw as the evil empire. Nineveh is the capital of the Assyrian empire, the empire that conquered the Northern Kingdom of Israel and exiled its people. Jonah is told to go to Nineveh to warn them that God's judgment is coming on them because of their "wickedness" (1:1–2). Of course, Jonah does not want to go because he wants God to destroy them. When Jonah finally does tell them of the coming judgment, they repent. When the king orders the whole city to repent, he tells the people to "turn from their evil ways and from the violence that is in their hands" (3:8). We get no more specific description of their wickedness and their evil ways. For our purposes, we don't need the specifics. The point is that God has moral expectations of all nations and their governments. God cares about the legal, economic, social, and military systems of even the enemies of Israel.

Our look at the audiences of the prophets shows that God has expectations of governments as well as of individuals. The prophets spoke to kings, rulers, judges, and others in places of power. They made it clear that God expects these people to craft systems that provide justice and mercy. At times, they call these leaders to offer special protections to people who are poor, even when they disadvantage those who are wealthy. Importantly, God does not have these expectations only for Israelite nations. The critiques of Amos and the accusations of Jonah show that God expects the laws and conduct of all nations to conform to the justice and mercy of God. It was not enough for the prophets to call individuals to act justly. The prophets demanded that government officials shape the economic, social, and judicial systems so that they reflect what God wants for the world, so that they reflect who God is.

Our glimpse into the world of the Hebrew prophets suggests that they expect the culture to be what God wants it to be. They seem to think it is possible to shape social and economic systems so that they reflect God's will. We may think this works best for a theocracy. If God is the true king, then all should conform to God's will. We, of course, do not see God as king in that sense. Even though we don't live in, or think we should have, a theocracy, these prophets can still teach us about how Christian values should shape national policy.

We see that these prophets believe that God expects all nations, not just the Israelite theocracy, to conform their laws and systems to God's will. Those demands commonly include providing justice for all and prohibiting (excessive) violence. The prophets say that God has such expectations for all leaders of all nations.

The direct statements that condemn leaders for not enforcing justice are powerful evidence for seeing God's expectations for nations. But the meaning of the call of Abraham and of Israel provides further grounding for thinking that God expects justice and mercy in all nations.

When God calls Abraham, God's intention is not just to bless Abraham. God says that Abraham and his descendants are to be a blessing to all the nations of the world (Gen 12:1–3). One way that the prophets think Israel lives out being a blessing to all people is that their nation is to be a light to the nations (Isa 42:6; 49:6). This means that the nation of Israel is to show others, including other nations, what God wants in the world. What God expects of Israel, then, is not meant to be an isolated case. The Israelite nations are to be the model that shows the rest of the world what God wants from the social and governmental systems of a nation.

Questions for Discussion

1. Why do you think the prophets chose to speak to the rulers of the nations? What benefit would they have by doing so? What disadvantages?

2. What does the regular prophetic focus on justice and the treatment of people who are poor tell you about God's concern for those issues?

3. We see that the prophets condemned foreign countries for failing to act justly toward people who are vulnerable. What does that suggest about God's expectations for all nations? What might it suggest about God's expectations for our nation's social and economic policies?

4. What does the story of Jonah say to us about God's concern for the ways nations conduct their business and social lives?

5. Read Psalm 72:1–4. What does this psalm—addressed to the king—expect of the government and its leader?

6. What does the prophets' focus on people in power say about God's expectations for the laws that govern our social and economic systems? What might that suggest about the church's involvement in discussions about social and economic policy?

7. What kinds of practices and laws might we have if we are working toward social and economic systems that reflect both the justice and the mercy of God?

4

Acts: The Earliest Church and Economic Systems

[T]hey would sell their possessions and goods and distribute
the proceeds to all, as any had need.

—Acts 2:45

As we saw in chapter 2, the Law was not concerned only about personal morality, but also with how the Israelites organized their social, economic, and political systems. We have also seen that the Hebrew prophets were convinced that God is concerned about the ways governments function, about the ways they treat both citizens and foreigners. And God was not concerned only about the policies of the Israelites' governments, but about the policies of all nations. In this chapter, we turn our attention to what the earliest church thought about God's concern for the ways economic and social systems work.

In chapter 3, we saw that the prophets seemed to think that people (even nations) were able to behave as God wants them to behave. But that confidence faded during the Babylonian exile and after the return from the exile. You can already see the doubts in the ways Genesis tells the stories of the fall and of Israel's ancestors; there are some unsavory tales about most of them. Even before the exile, Jeremiah was convinced that the people will never be able to live as God wants them to live. For him, the only solution was for God to make a new covenant that would include God changing the hearts of the people (33:31–34). Later writers would go so far as to talk about an evil inclination in the heart that keeps people from being able to live as they should (e.g., 2 Esd 3:20–22; 7:45–48).

This understanding of human nature led many within Judaism to look forward to a direct and worldwide act of God that would establish a just order. The Isaiah who wrote after the return from exile did not look for the restoration of the nation of Israel solely in Jerusalem and the region around it—he began to look for God's word to go out into the whole world (56:1–8; 60:1–18). These prophets and seers said it would take a dramatic and (literally) world-shaking act of God for the nations to act as God wanted them to act.

All New Testament writers held this more pessimistic view of the world. They lived in a world of empires shaped by the worship of many gods. Those gods did not demand the kind of society the Law and the prophets called for. Most members of the early church were not wealthy or powerful; remember that Jesus chose people like Peter, James, and John, children of small business owners who had no representation in governmental affairs. Most members of the early church came from places in society that did not have the power to influence the way social, political, and economic systems worked. But we can still see what the New Testament writers thought about God's will for the structure of society. To see what that will is, we have to talk about how they viewed the end times.

The Coming Kingdom

Jesus talked a lot about the coming of the kingdom of God. Many, probably most, first-century Jews would have heard that as a proclamation about God intervening to defeat the Romans and establish an independent Jewish state. But some may have thought he was proclaiming that world-shaking intervention we just talked about. It was the death and resurrection of Jesus that led his followers to think of the kingdom as that end-time event that would reshape the structures of the world. The resurrection of Jesus was a clear sign that the end of times had begun. After all, the resurrection of the dead happens at the end. But the resurrection of everyone did not follow immediately. Still, other things signaled that the church was living in the time of the kingdom. In Acts, we see Peter quoting the prophet Joel on the Day of Pentecost to say that the coming of the Spirit was a sign that the "last days" were here (2:17–21). The "last days" are the time when the kingdom begins to break into the world. Peter mentioned visions as another sign that the "last days" had come. The church also saw healings and speaking in tongues as signs that the kingdom was beginning to break into the world. These signs show that God is acting in the world in a new way.

Even as the early church proclaimed that it lived in the time of the kingdom, it was clear that the kingdom had not come in its fullness. Rome was still in charge and the world was no more just than before. So the people lived in two kingdoms at once. As believers in Christ, they participated in the kingdom of God, but they also had to accept the rule of Rome. In these circumstances, the church saw itself as the current and limited manifestation of the kingdom of God. As the current expression of the kingdom in the world, it was to be the place that lived by the values of God's kingdom. It was the place where God's will was supposed to be actualized. The church, as the partial entry of God's kingdom into the world, was to live by a different set of values than those seen in the religious, social, economic, and political systems of the Roman Empire. It is not that there were no common values, but the church was to hold to and promote values that the rest of the world rejected.

The differences were often dramatic. While one of the highest cultural values of the Greek and Roman worlds was gaining honor, church members said that honoring others above themselves was a core value. They put the good of others above their own good as a way of imitating Jesus, who put the good of others ahead of his good when he came to earth and was crucified.

The early chapters of Acts show us just how different a community looks when it adopts these alternative values. Here, Luke gives us his vision of the ideal church. We get to see what it would look like for the church to live fully as the manifestation of what God wants for the world. By chapter 5, however, the pressures and values of the outside world move people to lie about how much they put into the offering plate, and then people start complaining about not getting a fair share of the community's help. But we get this glimpse of the ideal:

> They devoted themselves to the apostles' teaching and fellowship, to the breaking of bread and the prayers. Awe came upon everyone, because many wonders and signs were being done by the apostles. All who believed were together and had

all things in common; they would sell their possessions and goods and distribute the proceeds to all, as any had need. Day by day, as they spent much time together in the temple, they broke bread at home and ate their food with glad and generous hearts, praising God and having the goodwill of all the people. And day by day the Lord added to their number those who were being saved. (Acts 2:42–47)

This is a powerful image of the beginning of the church. There are obvious experiences of God's power, daily fellowship meals, more people joining every day, and no fussing or complaining about fellow members. This is what it looks like to have the church serve in its fullest sense as the sign of what God wants in the world. One of the crucial elements of this kind of church life appears in verses 44–45. Luke says they have all things in common and sell their possessions to be able to give for the common good. While it may sound like they are starting a commune, that's not what's happening. We get to see more clearly what is going on in chapter 5, when it goes wrong. We get to see what the people are selling.

A Just Community

In chapter 5, Ananias and Sapphira sell some property to contribute to the church's communal fund. Others in the church had done this and given all the proceeds to the church. This couple decides to keep some of the money, but also to lie and say they gave it all. Peter knows the truth, and confronts Ananias when he says he is giving all he got for the property. Peter says that lying to him about this amounts to lying to God, and Ananias drops over dead. Sapphira is at home and does not know what has happened. When she comes to the church's meeting place, Peter confronts her; she tells the same lie and suffers the same fate.

There are troubling things about this story, but we want to notice that when this couple sold their property, they still had a home. This means that the property they sold was something other than the place where they lived. What they sold was most likely some kind of commercial property. It could have been an apartment building, but it was probably farmland. In the first century, a reliable way of investing wealth was to buy farmland. The way the system worked was that small farmers would get into debt they could not pay or would have a bad year that could not sustain them, and wealthy people would buy their farm and hire the farmer as a tenant farmer. The owner would take the profits and leave the farmer with less income than ever. This system increased the disparity between those who were rich and those who were poor. (It is not so unlike the way large corporations now buy farms in difficult financial times and then hire people to work on the land for much less than the farmer made before.)

This is the kind of land that members of the church are selling in Acts 2. Luke's description shows the church rejecting the Roman economic system. Wealthy church members sell the things that brought them economic advantage, and the church redistributes that wealth to its members in need. We see the same thing in Acts 4:32–37, where church members are again selling property and having the church distribute the money to those who have need.

We should note that members were not all treated the same. The wealthy people made sure that the economic needs of people who were poor were met. The price for meeting that need was that they divest themselves of the very thing that made them money. They took on economic disadvantage to address the economic inequities that were present in their world.

In Acts, this sharing of resources happens only within the church. But the church here is the place where God's Spirit is leading decisions; it is the embodiment of God's kingdom. It is, then, the model for what God wants for all the world. It is a glimpse of how economic and social systems would work if they were what God wants. This story is not just a story about rich people giving a bit of their money to help people who are poor. It is also a rejection of the first-century economic system. And it should be a challenge to ours. This story rejects the accumulation of wealth that comes through the exploitation of others. It rejects the system that has some people possessing more than they need while others have less than they need.

Acts does not have a pull-yourself-up-by-your-own-bootstraps frame of mind. Neither does it call for all people to get equal treatment. Richard Weiss, former dean of Lexington Theological Seminary, notes that when the prophets talk about justice, they do not mean that each person gets the same thing. Rather, they mean that the best interest of all in the community is served.[1] That is the kind of justice Acts sets up here. Acts sees this redistribution of wealth as God's will.

Seeking the Ideal

As we have seen, this ideal does not last long. By chapter 5, greed has damaged the community, and in chapter 6, there are complaints about the fund being distributed unfairly among the people who have need. Outside pressures break in on the ideal. Perhaps the economic system of the first century didn't allow the ideal to be sustainable long-term, and Luke does not say that any other church lived out the faith in this way. Still, this alternative system remains the ideal.

As the church today, we need to think about how this ideal might influence our life within the church and our positions and participation in the political arena. Luke has shown us something of God's will for the economic system, as well as for the church. We must remember that the church in Acts is to be a demonstration of what God wants for the whole world. It is the invasion of the kingdom into the territory that is governed and dominated by powers and systems that do not conform to God's will. The church is to be the sign of what God wants, and it is a means by which God's will is to spread in the world.

America's separation of church and state does not relieve the church of the task of caring about the social, cultural, and economic systems that govern the nation. Membership in the kingdom of God demands that we work to spread God's will in the world. Seeing the ideal for the church's use of wealth should shape the kinds of policies we support. It calls individual Christians and the church as a whole to support and work for economic policies and social programs that reflect what God wants for the world. It calls for the church to support and work for tax policies that seek economic justice of the kind we see in Acts. Such policies would require those who are wealthy to contribute more to the common good so that those who do not have enough can be helped. It calls the church to reject economic policies that give advantages to people who are wealthy and support policies that give advantages to people in need. If someone asks if such policies are trying to redistribute wealth, we can point to Acts as the teaching and example set by the apostles and the earliest church. If the church is to continue to be that sign of what God wants for the world, we can ask for nothing less.

Questions for Discussion

1. The earliest church was an organization that challenged the economic system of the Roman Empire. What might this suggest about the way they understood what Jesus said about the kingdom of God?

2. Over the last fifty years, it has been the practice of large corporate farms to wait for moments of distress in farm communities and then buy farms that are under severe financial strain. The farmer who then works the land is an employee who benefits far less from the profits of the crops. What do you think about comparing the Roman system of having wealthy people buy out small farmers and reducing their social status and income to the ways these contemporary corporate farms operate? How might they be similar? How might they be different? Do the usual practices of corporate farms fit with the values we see lived out in Acts 2?

3. How does the idea of the separation of church and state influence your views on the church's role in shaping economic and social policy? How might these policy discussions be similar to or different from moral laws (e.g., those against theft, murder, etc.) that are shaped by biblical values? How might it be different or similar to having our religious beliefs inform laws about abortion or marriage?

4. In what ways does this prioritization of the needs of people who are poor come into conflict with our western emphasis on individualism and on the need for people to "stand on their own two feet"?

5. Acts shows the early church upending an established practice of wealth generation. What systems are in place today that privilege wealth over economic justice? How might the church work to change systems around housing, banking, criminal justice, and education to build a more just society?

6. How might the church begin to live out some of the values we see in the first part of Acts? How might this example call the church to shape the community? What might it ask of individual members? What might the church do to shape economic policies?

7. What might it look like for the church to live out its identity as the place where others can see what God wants for the whole world?

5

Matthew's Jesus on the Church's Mission

You received without payment; give without payment.
—Matthew 10:8

In this chapter and the next, we will look at some of the teachings of Jesus as they appear in the Gospel of Matthew to see what they might say about the church's involvement in shaping the world around it. Matthew is Jewish, and he writes his Gospel for a church whose members are mostly Jewish. They continue to keep the Law as other Jews do and continue to be members of their local synagogues as well as believers in Christ. So, they attend the worship services of the church and the synagogue. Their claims about Jesus have made their lives in the synagogues difficult. Some have experienced persecution, at least in the form of being ostracized. Some seem to have been disowned by their families. Matthew writes to help them understand the situation they find themselves in and to help them think about how to live as the church in that place. This Gospel wants to assure them that they have made the right decision about Christ and that God will vindicate their faithfulness.

We will look at some texts that speak to the place of the church in the world, God's judgment on the wicked, God's judgment of nations, and God's promises for the faithful. The four texts we will explore in this chapter and the next are all among the lectionary readings for Year A in the period after Pentecost. This means that these are among the texts that many churches hear often. I think they have much to say about how the church should seek to be involved in things beyond religious matters.

Matthew 9:35–10:8

This section of Matthew is the story of Jesus first sending the disciples out to proclaim the coming of the kingdom of heaven. Before we get to this story, Jesus has preached the Sermon on the Mount and his ministry is going strong. Matthew tells of Jesus traveling around healing and teaching. The passage at hand begins with a summary of that healing and teaching and has Jesus grieving over the amount of need he sees around him. He tells the disciples to pray that God will send workers. Then he appoints twelve of his followers to be those workers. In 10:1, Matthew calls them *disciples*, those who follow and learn; in verse 2, he calls them *apostles*, those who are sent with a mission to accomplish. Jesus gives them power to exorcise demons, heal the sick, and meet the needs he's seen, and he sends them out to use it.

The message they are to proclaim is that "the kingdom of heaven is near" (10:7). When Matthew talks about the kingdom of heaven, he does not mean some otherworldly thing.

It is his usual way of referring to the kingdom of God. Using "heaven" is a way to avoid referring to God directly. Many Jews of the first century avoided direct references to God to make sure they did not take God's name in vain. Matthew reflects that practice.

The proclamation that the kingdom is near has two different shades of meaning. Saying that it is "near" could mean that it will come soon. Or "near" could mean that it is in close proximity. Matthew probably wants hearers to think of both. When Jesus or the apostles are close by, the kingdom is near. At the same time, their proclamation means that God is about to do a new thing. So, the kingdom is close by and the time is nearly here for God to bring it more fully into the world.

In Matthew, proclamations of the coming of the kingdom are usually accompanied by calls to repent and warnings about judgment. But not here. In this whole section there is no mention of sin or the need for repentance. Instead, the mission Jesus gives these apostles is to heal the sick, raise the dead, cleanse lepers, and exorcise demons. The emphasis here is on healing those who are suffering. The disciples are sent to move the world closer to what God wants it to be, a place where there is no suffering and death, a place where evil is no longer imposed from outside (what Matthew called demon possession); their mission is a sign of what it will look like when the kingdom comes.

Matthew sets up this first mission of the apostles as a pattern for the church. He wants the church to take up the mission Jesus gave the apostles. The church is to proclaim the nearness of the kingdom—in both senses. And the church is to work to make the world what God wants it to be, what God will make it when the kingdom is fully present. After all, Jesus had already taught his disciples to pray, "Your will be done, on earth as it is in heaven" (6:10).

So how does the church today adopt this Jesus-given pattern of its presence and work in the world? We obviously cannot heal miraculously. But the church can work to alleviate suffering and pain. This commission from Christ demands that the church work to eradicate the effects of demonic forces. These demonic forces today, as then, include the powers that keep injustice in our economic, social, educational, and judicial systems. The church can do the work this passage demands by helping to create structures and laws that relieve the suffering and pain that our cultural systems impose, especially on the people who are vulnerable. This is the first mission Christ gives the apostles; this is a mission the church is to continue.

We should notice that this is not a call to get converts. Matthew certainly believes in that, but it's not the point here. The first task the apostles are given is to make the world the kind of place God wants it to be, to defeat those things that grieve Jesus as he looks at the world. Matthew thinks of making converts as a part of making the world what God wants it to be, as the Great Commission shows. Gaining converts is part of the program because living as Jesus teaches helps make the kind of world God wants, as people treat one another with respect and dignity. But according to this text, alleviating the suffering of the sick and those oppressed by outside evil forces is also a central task.

We might note here that Jesus tells the disciples not to take this message to gentiles or Samaritans, but only to Jews. It seems that establishing God's will for the world starts by establishing it within the people of God. It is within the people of God that we can catch a glimpse of the vision of life God wants for all. It is with that vision that they can then be empowered to move out to share it with all people. But the next time Jesus sends the apostles out, it is to the whole world.

Matthew 10:32–39

Our second text from Matthew is also part of the sending of the apostles on their first mission. Jesus is giving instructions and telling them what they will face. As we discuss this passage, remember that most people in Matthew's church are Jewish and are experiencing persecution because of their belief in Christ as Savior. In 10:17, Jesus warns his followers that people will turn them in to the ruling council and that they will receive physical punishment for their faith. Synagogues were able to punish errant members by beating them with a rod. (Paul endured this multiple times; see 2 Cor 11:24.) Some members of Matthew's church may have suffered that punishment. Others may have been banned from their synagogues. Most persecution of the church in the first century was economic and social persecution, which could be severe. After all, if people refuse to do business with you, that might mean sending your kids to bed hungry. If people stopped associating with you, you lost crucial social support. Plus, by the time Matthew was written, Rome was looking at the church with more suspicion and had executed some of its members.

Matthew 10:32–39 is part of a section of warnings about persecution. In this instance, the persecutions come from family members who are turning on each other, perhaps bringing charges against one another. Jesus says throughout the larger section (10:16–42) that those who believe in him should expect to suffer just as he suffered. He tells them not to be afraid of people who can kill them, but rather to be afraid of God, who can send them to agonizing punishment.

Our passage follows that implicit threat with a straightforward threat: Those who deny Jesus in this world will be denied by Christ at judgment. Jesus says he has not come to bring peace, but conflict—conflict even within families. He finishes by saying that loyalty to him must be greater than loyalty to parents and children.

This is a hard text no matter how things are going in the world. Can you imagine what we would say if our pastor stood up and advised children, including grown children, to disregard what their parents think and the values they hold? Those of us in mainline churches often see ourselves as those who hold together the values of both the culture and the church. We want to see ourselves as those who can preserve the best of both worlds. Jesus seems to say here that this stance is impossible.

In the flow of this section of Matthew, Jesus has emphasized the importance of disciples owning their faith publicly; they must confess him before others. He says their salvation depends on it. It is on the heels of this demand that he says he is not bringing peace, but conflict. This is not because Jesus prefers conflict, but because the values and social and economic systems of the world oppose what God wants for the world. Adopting the beliefs and values of the kingdom brings believers into conflict with those who hold the values that make the world work as it does. Jesus says that holding to the values of the kingdom splits families. The members of Matthew's church already know this to be true.

While Jesus is talking most directly about confessing belief in who he is, what he has already said in Matthew shows that he demands that believers adopt a different way of being and evaluating all things. A quick scan of the Beatitudes (5:1–12) shows clearly that Jesus's values and those of the world around him are radically different. He says that the meek will inherit the earth, but how often do you see someone get a raise for being meek? Chapter 10 shows Jesus rejecting any cozying up to cultural values, even when it involves relations with family members.

When we read about these conflicts between parents and children, we should not just think of pre-teens and adolescents. In the first century, children remained under the authority of the head of the household all their lives. Men were expected to defer to their fathers in business and personal matters. Women were under the control of their fathers until they married. Then they were under the power of their husband, who was under the power of his father. One Roman writer boasts that a father can have his son executed even if his son has become an important government official. Things were less stringent in Palestine, but lifetime deference was still expected. It is the way children honored their parents, as the Ten Commandments demand.

This cultural arrangement created great problems for Matthew's church. Some, perhaps many, joined and remained members of the church against the will of their parents. As synagogues began to condemn the beliefs of the church, this seems to have led families of church members to pressure those believers to leave the church. This led to significant ruptures in family relationships as children turned against their parents and parents against their children. This was made even more serious by the connections between the household and the family business. The household was often the location of the family business. If, as may have been the case often, the son remained in the family business, being disowned by his father might leave him without a job or any economic security. Clearly, this kind of conflict could have devastating effects.

So, what is a church member to do? Should they conform to societal expectations and honor their parents, or should they stay in the church? Should they honor their parents or follow Jesus? Matthew has just told his readers that Jesus says those who deny him will lose their salvation. Soon, Matthew will tell the story of Jesus turning away his own family and calling his disciples his true family (12:46–50). Matthew requires his audience to make the same choice. If they face losing their families because of their faith, they must follow the example of Jesus and allow themselves to be cut off from their families.

For most of us today, church membership rarely means we will be alienated from our families, at least not to that degree. But we should not lose the point: Following Christ makes stringent demands. Those demands include rejecting the judgments and values of the society and culture that surrounds us. Sometimes it's easy to recognize the conflicts between what God wants for the world and our social, cultural, economic, and political views and values. Sometimes it is hard. But the conflict is always there. What counts as success in our culture seldom looks like the self-giving love we see in the life and death of Jesus. What our economic and political systems claim is good is seldom consistent with taking up one's cross and following Jesus.

Speaking out against the systems that dominate the world and the nation is risky business. Just ask the members of Matthew's church. And Jesus knows it can get you killed. But he says not to be afraid of those who can kill you. Think rather of the God who gives true life. The call to stand against family is a stark demand from Jesus, but it is a demand. In spite of how harsh it sounds, Jesus says that opposing the world—even when that includes our families—to confess him and what he wants for the world can give life.

In this text we see that living the faith is not just a private thing that we do at home or in church. Being disciples of Jesus requires Christians to stand publicly for what God wants for the world. That public stand will put us in conflict with the cultural systems of our time, even perhaps with our families. But in this text and in the rest of Matthew, that is what Jesus demands.

Questions for Discussion

1. What does it say about the mission of Jesus when we see that he sends out his disciples on their first mission and gives no instructions about making converts? What does this say to you about the mission of the church?

2. How do you think this first mission of healing and relieving suffering relates to the church's mission to bring people to confess Christ as Savior?

3. In Matthew 10:17–18, Jesus says that when the apostles undertake their mission, they will be dragged before governors and kings. Why do you think the message he sends them with is a threat to governing authorities?

4. According to this teaching of Jesus, what reactions should the church expect if it stands up for what God wants for the world? How might this teaching

relate to those who say we should not "bring politics" into the church? Why is it a problem to do that?

5. What might the public confession of Christ that this text calls for look like today? That confession was such that it drew the attention of governmental officials in Matthew's day. How might a full confession like the one Jesus is talking about here bring the church into conflict with the laws that govern various aspects of our nation?

6. What might that public confession of Christ lead us to work for in the area of healthcare? Prison reform? Sentencing laws? Tax policy? Banking regulations?

6

Expectations for Nations in Parables of Jesus

All the nations will be gathered before him . . .
—Matthew 25:32

In the last chapter, we saw how Jesus called his disciples to care for the physical well-being of people in the world. We also saw that he knew that living by the values he taught would bring his followers into conflict with the values of the world around them. In this chapter, we turn our attention to two parables in which Jesus speaks of God's judgment over the whole world, including those who are not in the church.

Matthew 13:24–30

The parable of the Weeds among the Wheat is a difficult text in Matthew. It is part of a section that highlights the conflicts between Jesus and the people who reject him (12:36–13:[52 or] 58). Jesus's telling of the parable comes after his interpretation of the Parable of the Sower (13:1–9). After this parable, Jesus tells two more before interpreting this one. When the interpretation does come, Jesus explains that the parable means that those who oppose the will of God face condemnation that includes "weeping and gnashing of teeth" (13:42).

The parable of Weeds among the Wheat puts opposing Jesus and his will in cosmic terms and sets it in the context of end-time judgment. In this setting, the parable has only two kinds of people, the "children of the kingdom" who do God's will and the "children of the evil one" who oppose God's will. At the end, Christ ("the son of man") sends the angels to gather the wicked people out of "his kingdom" (v. 41). This is unusual language for the Gospels. The "kingdom" usually refers to the church and the realm where the will of God is done. This means that most of the world is outside the kingdom of God. But when this parable ends, it is the judgment day, the time when Christ's reign is fully established over the whole world. So, all the world has become "his kingdom."

This parable has good news and bad news. The bad news is that the conflict between good and evil lasts until the end of time. The parable has God allow the evil to remain so that growth of the good will not be stunted. Perhaps that means it is possible for at least some of the "children of the evil one" to become "children of the kingdom." But the main point is that believers should expect evil to persist and to fight for dominance. On the other hand, the good news is that God promises that justice will prevail and the will of God will triumph, as we see in the growth of the wheat.

Still, the final defeat of evil does not happen until Judgment Day.

This parable clearly sees the final defeat of evil as something only God can accomplish. Since God does that at the judgment, evil remains in the world until its end. The persistence of evil is not, however, a reason for acquiescence. Judgment will mean eradicating evil and vindicating righteousness. That means that the righteous can make sacrifices for the advancement of God's will in the present. Matthew intends this parable to encourage his persecuted church. They are encouraged to be faithful, as the parable assures them of the faithfulness of God. Jesus knows that evil will persist, yet he dies for the good of others. He can do that because he trusts that in the ultimate accounting, God will make things right. That trust is vindicated in the resurrection of Christ. His resurrection, then, is the church's assurance that working against evil, working against injustice, is doing the will of God and that God will reward that work.

This reminder of the promise that the purposes of God will eventually reign should give the church courage to work for what God wants in the world now. This parable tells us that we should not be surprised to find that some people around us oppose God's will. It also should not discourage us. While it may seem that evil and injustice get stronger at times, this parable asserts that such resurgences will ultimately be overcome by the will of God. When our best efforts to do good seem overwhelmed or defeated, this parable promises that we are working for what will be vindicated; it promises that the good God intends for the world will be the final state of things.

In this parable, Christians are the "children of the kingdom." That identity brings responsibility. The children of the kingdom are supposed to live in ways that reflect their identity. That is, Christians' lives are to exemplify what the kingdom stands for. This parable does not spell out how the children of the kingdom are to act. But we can be sure that they are to live in ways that are consistent with the values and outlook of the coming kingdom. Note that in this parable the Son of Man reigns over all the world, not just the church. This suggests that it is the job of the children of the kingdom to be working for what God wants in all the world. Christians can draw hope from this parable as they remember that God's justice and love are the final word for the world and all of reality. This can encourage us to work for a world that reflects God's justice and for a culture that embodies God's love. It can give us the courage to evaluate candidates and policies by whether they stand for what God wants for the world. Faithfulness to our identity as children of the kingdom requires us to oppose those who do not work for God's justice and love for all people.

Matthew 25:31–46

Our last text from Matthew is the well-known parable of the Judgment. It is commonly said to show that the church should be engaged in taking care of people who are poor and in need. But, as we will see, this parable is not directly about what the church should do. Still, what we find in this parable does have important implications for the church's life and its engagement with social, political, and economic systems.

Matthew gives us five sections in which Jesus stops his travels and healings to simply teach. When he is finished teaching, Jesus is again on the move. The fifth teaching section (or Discourse, as these sections are often called) is 24:3–25:46. All the teaching in this section is about the end-time judgment. It includes several parables, and this reading is the last of them. All of the parables before this one have been about what church members need to do to be ready for the final judgment. They stress that believers always need to be ready for it. They stay ready by being faithful to the tasks that disciples are given.

But this last parable is different. It is not a warning to the church. Instead, this judgment scene has Christ bring before him "all the nations" (25:32). The word translated as "nations" here in Matthew is *ethnē*. It is the Greek term used throughout Matthew's Gospel to speak of gentiles (e.g., 4:15; 6:32; 10:5, 18; 21:43; and 24:7, 9, 14). It is the usual Greek word that the New Testament uses to talk about gentiles. This follows one of the usual uses of the term among first-century Jews. They used it to refer to gentiles—that is, to all non-Jews. But it is also the general Greek word for "nations." If Matthew is using it as he typically does, this is a reference to gentiles generally, but it is possible that it is a more specific reference to governments.

In either case, Matthew shows us that Jesus has turned from talking about how church members will be judged to talking about the judgment of outsiders. We should remember again that most members of Matthew's church were Jewish. By the time Matthew wrote this, his church had been persecuted not only by fellow Jews, but also by the Roman government. The Romans had destroyed the temple in Jerusalem and much of the city. The Romans viewed all Jews with suspicion and Jewish members of the church with even more. By the time of this writing, Rome had executed church members (including Peter and Paul) and there had been spurts of regional governmental per-secution of the church. Given all these things, members of

Matthew's church were wondering what God's response to their suffering would be. What was God going to do to the people persecuting them? Matthew includes this parable as a way to answer such questions.

Here, Jesus speaks about God's response to the pain inflicted on the church by outsiders, by gentiles, perhaps in the form of their governing powers. While it seems odd, this is not the only place in Matthew that envisions a separate judgment for gentiles. In 19:28, Jesus tells the twelve disciples that they will serve as judges over the tribes of Israel. The idea that Jews and gentiles are judged separately has its roots in the Hebrew prophets. Ezekiel envisions a time when God blesses Israel and demonstrates God's judgment before the nations (Ezek 39:21–24). After all, Israel had the duty to keep a covenant that gentiles were not a part of. By the first century, the idea that there would be a separate judgment for gentiles was a common theme that we see in books that are now in the Apocrypha and other Jewish writings (see, for example, 1 En 9:14; Psalm of Solomon 17:29; 2 Esd 13:33–49). In 2 Baruch, a book that was written a few years after Matthew, the fate of nations in this separate judgment is determined by how they treated Israel (13:1–14:2).

In Matthew's account of this separate judgment, the fate of the gentiles/nations is determined by how they treat church members. This is seen clearly in verse 40, where Jesus talks about how they treated the "least of my brothers." Throughout Matthew, when Jesus talks about "brothers" and when he talks about the "little ones," he is always talking about his disciples. That is also the case here. In this judgment scene, the judgment of the people outside the church is based on how they have treated people in the church.

All of the things mentioned that the gentiles/nations either do or don't do involve taking care of the physical needs of suffering church members. When we remember that Matthew's church was being persecuted, we can see how important this scene is. In this judgment, God rejects and punishes the people who ignore the physical needs of church members. This was important for a church enduring persecution to hear. It means that those who impose suffering on them would not get away with it. But even more, the people who fail to intervene to help them are also condemned. It is not enough to refrain from being the persecutor. The only way to receive God's blessing is to be one who actively intervenes to alleviate their suffering. If, in the midst of suffering, it seems that God doesn't care, this judgment scene shows that God will make sure that justice is done.

We noted at the beginning of this chapter that this parable is often read as one addressed to the church. We have seen, however, that it is really about nonbelievers and perhaps their governments. Since that is the case, we have to think about what it says to the church. Since it addresses the behavior of nonbelievers, it gives us a glimpse at what God expects of all human beings. It tells of the way God will judge people who do not believe that God is God. God expects that nonbelievers know it is their responsibility to take care of the physical needs of church members who are facing a lack of food, clothing, shelter, and comfort. Notably, the condemned in this passage are not the persecutors. They are not the people who inflict the troubles. The condemned are the people who ignore the created need and so fail to help. God expects nonbelievers to actively respond to the needs of God's people.

If this is what God expects of nonbelievers, we can be

sure that God expects more of God's people. Church members know of and experience the benefits of the self-giving love of Christ, something the nonbelievers have not accepted. If we have experienced this kind of grace, it should be nearly impossible not to give to others. Jesus has already told his disciples that his life of serving others, which includes dying for others, is the example of the way they are to live (20:24–28). This service to others includes serving their physical needs. God expects more and greater expressions of care for those who need food, shelter, and support from the people who know and have been blessed by Jesus. And God expects that providing this care will extend beyond the walls of the church and out into the world. We saw in our treatment of Matthew 9:35–10:8 that Jesus sent the disciples out to offer healing and help among the people of God. But we also saw that Jesus called the disciples to spread the good news of what God wants for all people to the whole world.

As we noted above, Matthew may well have had governments as well as individuals in mind here. If Matthew had individuals in mind, then he expected nonbelievers to defy the empire to help church members. But since Matthew's church had suffered at the hands of the Roman Empire, Matthew may have also been including it here. If so, then this judgment scene speaks directly to what God expects of governments and their policies. The expectation Jesus sets forth is that they feed and clothe those who are poor and sick and those who are immigrants. Jesus even expects that prisons will not be oppressive, but will rather provide the services imprisoned people need.

Perhaps this statement about coming to see imprisoned people makes it more likely that Jesus has people rather than government authorities directly in view. (That will not be the case when we get to Revelation.) Even so, this passage has inescapable implications for what God expects governments to do. Since governments are the organized ways that people structure how they treat one another, the people in charge are expected to create systems that exhibit the values God demands of each person.

This scene of the judgment of nonbelievers gives the church a clear mandate. The church is to work to alleviate suffering and physical need for all people. To do so is simply doing what God expects of nonbelievers. The work of addressing the needs of those who are hungry, those who are in need of housing, and those who are immigrants (strangers) goes beyond offering aid once people find themselves in difficult situations. It must include working for systems that are more just and that allow for more mercy so that those circumstances are eradicated, or at least minimized. Matthew's church was not in a position to influence how the government functioned. But its lack of power is not an excuse for today's church to refuse or neglect to use its social and political power to move policies and laws toward the justice God wants for the world. To ignore the task of working for just social and economic systems is to place ourselves under the condemnation of those who did not help those needy church members in this passage.

Questions for Discussion

1. It can be discouraging to hear that evil will remain in the world until its end. How might Matthew's assurance that God's will and justice will ultimately prevail give you encouragement to continue to work for God's will in the world?

2. Does being assured that you will participate in the ultimate victory of God's will and justice give you encouragement to continue to work for God's will in the world? Why or why not?

3. In the parable of the Weeds among the Wheat, Jesus speaks of God's kingdom as including the whole world. What might that eventual reign of Christ suggest about how Christians should participate in the world today? Would it suggest involvement in shaping the world, withdrawal from trying to shape it, or something else?

4. The parable of the Weeds among the Wheat calls those who believe in Christ "children of the kingdom." What kinds of responsibilities might living out this identity bring to us in the present, when Christ is not yet reigning over the world? Given that Christ came into the world to show it the love and will of God, how might this identity move us to show God's will and love to the world today? How would living as a child of the kingdom shape what we think about social or economic programs to help people who are poor?

5. Given that the parable of the Great Judgment is about the judgment of non-Christians and may be about the behavior of governments, what does

Christ expect to see in governmental policies toward and programs for people who are disadvantaged and poor in a democratic nation?

6. What does this parable that tells about how nonbelievers will be judged say about the church's involvement in developing the social and economic policies of a nation?

7. How might the parable of the judgment of the nations influence our thinking about the separation of church and state?

7

Luke and Care for Those Who Are Poor and Disadvantaged

He has sent me to proclaim release to the captives and recovery of sight to the blind, to let the oppressed go free.

—Jesus in Luke 4:18

In the last two chapters, I have focused attention on what Matthew has to say about how or whether believers should use their faith to shape the social and economic systems that govern the world. I noted that these are lectionary texts, but that is not the only reason I gave them so much attention. I also wanted us to think about the Matthew texts because when people talk about Jesus and social issues, they nearly always turn to Luke. Luke is the Gospel that gives more attention to outcasts and people who are seen as second class than the other Gospels do. (We will take notice of how Luke does that shortly.) But if we focus only on Luke when we talk about the place of Christians and the church in shaping policies and laws, it may sound as though what he says is just one of the ways the gospel can move into the world, with the other Gospels giving us different paths. It is certainly true that the four Gospels give us different interpretations of Jesus. But Jesus challenges the social, political, and economic systems of the first century in all of them. It is a disservice to focus only and always on Luke; still, we don't want to leave him out.

A Gospel for the Forgotten

Luke believed that one of the main purposes of the ministry of Jesus was to restore the value and dignity of people who were regarded as second class. Jesus works to make it clear that they are as valuable as any other of God's children. To make this point, we see Jesus privileging the good of such people. You can see how Luke privileges poor people and those considered second class even in the way he tells the story of Jesus's birth. We can look first at who the angel visits to tell about the birth of Jesus. In Matthew the angel visits only Joseph, but in Luke he visits only Mary. This is an example of Luke making the role of women more prominent in the stories he tells. Then, Matthew has the Magi visit the baby Jesus. These travelers are wealthy enough and are on a high enough rung of the social structure that they can get an immediate meeting with the king. These characters do not appear in Luke. Instead, the people who get the news of Jesus's birth and come to see him are third-shift shepherds who are probably just hired hands. And it is only in Luke that Jesus is born in a barn. In Luke's telling, beginning with Jesus's birth, the people who know about him are those lower in the social order. Luke will continue this trend by having Jesus focus his ministry on those who are poor and disadvantaged.

The parables of Jesus that appear only in Luke also tell of the importance of the people on whom proper society looks down. The parable of the Good Samaritan (10:25–37) is shocking not just because the religious people don't help, but also because of who does. First-century Jews looked down on Samaritans because of their ethnic identity and their improper worship of God. But when a good observant Jew asks Jesus how to have eternal life, Jesus says, "Go be like a Samaritan." That would have been taken as an insult. Yet Jesus takes the ethnic group that good people look down on and makes one of its number the hero of the story. In doing so, Jesus rejects the social system that declares Samaritans to be less than equal. By extension, Jesus rejects every social system that considers any ethnic group to be less than equal. Given that Jesus calls would-be disciples to take up their crosses and follow him, this story also requires all believers to reject and fight against such systems.

I will mention just one other parable, that of the Rich Man and Lazarus (Luke 16:19–31). I have to admit that I really don't like this parable. It just seems to go too far, especially in what it says about how God deals with wealthy people. The first thing to notice about this parable is its name; we know the name of the wrong person. In both ancient and modern narratives, the nameless are always the people who are poor or those considered second class. But here, we know only the name of the homeless man. It is the identity of the rich man that is blotted out through neglecting to mention it, rather than that of the poor person. That's not the bad part! Read the parable over carefully. What does it say that the rich person did wrong? We will say he was condemned because he neglected Lazarus, but the parable doesn't say that. There is no description of anything that might have caused this man's damnation except that he is rich. We can say all kinds of things about him not using his money to help the person who was poor and right in front of him, but Luke does not. He writes that the rich man is damned because he had things good in this life (see v. 25). This should make most of us very uncomfortable. It violates all sorts of standards we hold dear. We think God rewards hard work with riches, or at least that being rich is a good thing. Luke wants us to rethink that.

Perhaps we can take some comfort in noting that there are rich people in the church in Acts (which is also written by Luke). So, all rich people are not automatically damned. But Luke is sure that wealth is dangerous. In Acts the wealthy church members have obligations to help those who have less and to support the work that God wants done in the world (see chapter 4 of this book).

In case these parables don't show the danger of wealth clearly enough, Luke spells it out explicitly in multiple places. Like Matthew and Mark, Luke includes Jesus's words about how hard it is for rich people to enter the kingdom. When a wealthy person refuses to sell everything and follow Jesus, Jesus says it is harder for a rich person to be saved than it is for a camel to go through the eye of a needle (Luke 18:24–25). Some interpreters have said there was a gate in the wall of Jerusalem called the Eye of the Needle because it was low and camels had to get on their knees to get through. That would have made the entrance challenging, but the rich could still get in. In truth, there was no such gate. The point of the eye-of-the-needle analogy is that it is impossible for the rich to be saved. The disciples understood the point immediately and responded by asking, "Who then can be saved?" They assume the rich will be saved because they already have blessings from God. But they are wrong. Jesus explains that while it is humanly impossible for the rich to be saved, God can save them (18:26–27).

The Political Implications of the Gospel

While three of the Gospels tell that particular parable in a similar way, there are many other places where Luke's telling of a story shows Jesus favoring people considered outcasts and second class in ways the other Gospels do not. Matthew, Mark, and Luke all tell the story of Jesus returning home to preach in Nazareth. Matthew and Mark place the story in the middle of Jesus's ministry in Galilee, where it makes good chronological sense. Jesus had become famous and then came back to his home synagogue to preach. But Luke moves the story, making it the first story in the ministry of Jesus. He also expands the story. These moves make it the theme-setting story for Jesus's ministry. Only Luke has Jesus stand up in the synagogue and read the text from Isaiah that says that the Spirit is upon him so that he preaches good news to the poor, proclaims release to prisoners, and heals the sick. After reading the scroll, Jesus says that is happening now, in him (4:16–21). This is good news to an audience oppressed by the Romans. But Jesus then makes it clear that the nice people at the synagogue are not the people this promise is talking about. Rather it is the people they look down on, those they are glad are not at services that day. The dispossessed and hurting people are central in Jesus's ministry. Poor people are his special focus, and he identifies at least one political implication of his ministry, the release of people in prison.

I will mention just one other place where Luke makes the oppressed and disadvantaged the special focus of what the gospel will do: Mary's song during her visit to Elizabeth (1:46–55). We often read the Magnificat and pass over some of what it says about what God is doing through Christ. It contains significant promises for the oppressed, but also significant threats to the powerful. In verses 51–53, Mary says that God, who has great power, knows the arrogant thoughts of "their" hearts. We hear who "they" are in the next two verses. Here God throws kings off their thrones and raises the humble to power and gives abundant gifts to those who are poor while sending away the wealthy people with nothing. Part of what God intends to do through Jesus is to reverse the status of those who are wealthy and those who are poor. God rejects the system that privileges and honors those who are wealthy.

We should not miss that it is kings who are deposed in verse 52. That means that the work of Christ has political implications. The same is true at the crucifixion. Crucifixion was not the way regular murderers, heretics, and other criminals were executed. It was far too much work for that. Crucifixion was a political execution. It was reserved for insurrectionists and others who challenged Roman rule. It was in those cases that the empire needed to set an example. Notice that the charges the Sanhedrin makes against Jesus are political. He misleads the people, they say, by telling them not to pay taxes and by claiming to be a king. Following this charge, Pilate's question to Jesus is not about religion, it is "Are you the king of the Jews?" (Luke 23:1–3). In all four Gospels, Jesus is executed on a political charge.

That's not just because it was the only way for the Jerusalem leaders to frame their case. For Luke's audience, the execution of Jesus fits in with the overall theme of his life and ministry. The song of Mary had already said that he would be a threat to kings. In addition, when Luke calls Jesus the Son of God, he puts Jesus in the line of the kings of Israel. This title points to the significance of that name when it was used for the kings of Israel (e.g., Ps 2:7). When the angel tells Mary she will have a child, the angel says that God will give Jesus the throne of his father David and that his kingdom will never end (1:32–33). Luke does not think of Christ's reign as just a religious kingdom or as one that is in heaven. Luke looks for Christ to reign over all things, everywhere. This puts Jesus in conflict with the Roman Empire from the very beginning.

Extending the Reign of Christ

One of the ways Luke shows this conflict is in the ways Jesus challenges the economic system. As is always the case, social status and wealth are connected. In the first century, a central part of the socio-economic structure was the patronage system. In this system, accepting a gift brought the expectation of a reciprocal gift. While gifts were often given to people in the same social class, often a wealthy person gave an initial gift to the less wealthy person. The original gift might be a business loan or a banquet invitation, or any type of gift. This system of gift giving established a relationship that included the obligation of giving a gift in return. When these gifts were exchanged among social peers, it meant that the wealthy people entertained one another and strengthened ties with those of their own social class, which meant keeping the wealth among themselves.

Of course, these relationships were often not between social peers. Even almsgiving was seen as an act that created a relationship. Of course, a monetary gift to a person of less status could not be matched with money. Instead, this obligation might be met by being a part of the patron's entourage when he goes to meetings, social events, or public events. Or one might fulfill the obligation by getting others in your group, maybe your trade guild, to vote the way your patron wanted them to vote. There were many ways to respond to the obligation a gift imposed, and a good response usually meant the person would receive another gift. This system often helped both parties, but it was structured so that it was more advantageous for the wealthier person. The more clients (people who owed you a gift) a patron gained, the more social and political power that patron accumulated.

Jesus explicitly rejects this system. While attending a banquet of a wealthy person, he says that when those who are wealthy have a banquet, they should not invite those who are able to invite them back. Instead they should invite the people who are disadvantaged, sick, and poor. He says they should invite the people who cannot repay them. It is gift giving with no expectation of obligation that Jesus says will be repaid in the resurrection (14:12–14). Jesus says they must reject the expectations of the economic system to please God. But Jesus goes even further. In the Sermon on the Plain (Luke's equivalent of Matthew's Sermon on the Mount), Jesus tells the audience that they should loan money to people who they know cannot pay it back. The wealthy people are to lend without expectation of repayment. They are to do this so that their economic conduct reflects the mercy of God (6:34–36).

With the exception of his trial and his debates with temple officials in the last week of his life, Jesus does not address his teaching to government officials. He did not have the standing to be able to get an appointment with them. But acknowledging that Jesus spoke to private individuals should not lead us to think that he didn't think his teaching should shape social and economic policies. When Jesus denounces people who take advantage of the economic system to gain wealth by legally taking the property of the disadvantaged (here widows, 20:45–47), it is also a judgment on the system that allows the abuse. The two are inseparable. What he says about banking (who you loan money to) shows that the economic system is to reflect who God is. God's people are to shape it so that it reflects the mercy of God. While he is in the temple, Jesus's opponents ask him how the faithful should relate to the empire, specifically as it relates to paying taxes (20:20–26). They ask it as a trick question, but Jesus gives a demanding answer. When he says, "give to emperor the things that are the emperor's, and to God the things that are God's," he is not telling them to cooperate with Rome. Rather, he is making the point that everything they have is God's. That means that the way they participate in the political and economic systems is to be controlled by the knowledge that they are using what belongs to God.

It is important to remember that Luke presents Jesus as the son of David who will reign forever. As I noted above, Luke does not think that the reign of Jesus is only in heaven. It is a reign that intends to take down the rulers and the powerful. It rejects the ways they have been governing. The images of Jesus at God's right hand in Acts (e.g., Acts 7:56) show that Luke believes that the reign of Christ has begun. The point of having Christ as king is that he will make all things reflect what God wants. His rule is not yet fully effective on earth, but its work of removing unjust rulers has begun. That reign is to be realized in the church—and the church, as the people who have Christ as king, is to try to extend that reign into the rest of the world.

The teaching of Jesus in Luke has clear implications for how the church extends Christ's reign in the world. His reign demands changes to economic systems so that advantages are given to the people who are poor and disadvantaged rather than to the wealthy and powerful. Instead of lending without expectation of repayment, banks now give lower rates to people who qualify for bigger loans (just check on the rates for home equity loans). Of course, banks that don't expect any repayment of any loans can't stay in business. But Luke's Jesus calls for more than a system that treats people the same. He calls for an economic system that includes mercy.

Questions for Discussion

1. What would the teaching of Jesus about giving loans to those who cannot repay say about payday loan companies? How do you imagine the church shaping laws relating to them based on the Jesus we have seen in Luke?

2. Can you imagine an economic system that reflects both the justice of God and the mercy of God? What role might the church have in creating a just and merciful economic system?

3. What do these examples from Luke's Gospel suggest about the way individuals are to treat people who are poor and disadvantaged? What do they suggest about the role Christians can have in changing the systems that harm or disadvantage people?

4. How might the Magnificat challenge you to think differently about systems and structures of power?

5. Certain laws allow wealthy people or institutions to take possession of or repossess the property of people who are poor and disadvantaged. How might following the way of Jesus affect whether or not Christians take advantage of such laws? How might these laws be changed to reflect God's mercy? What might the teaching of Jesus suggest about the role of the church in creating this kind of change?

6. Jesus clearly says in Luke that people who are poor and disadvantaged are to be given preferential treatment in the way the economic system works. What place does God's justice have in this demand? What place does God's mercy have in this demand?

7. How could the demand for preferential treatment of people who are poor and disadvantaged shape social policies? Economic policies? Government funding priorities? Hiring policies?

8

Paul, the Ruler of This World, and Sin (with a Capital S)

Do you not know that if you present yourselves to anyone as obedient slaves, you are slaves of the one whom you obey?

—Romans 6:16

Romans is both beautiful and difficult. It has wondrous descriptions of salvation and of God's presence with believers, and it has consternating comments about human nature and about the law. This is the case, in part, because it is trying to accomplish a complicated task. Paul is introducing himself to a church he has never visited, wanting them to accept him as their apostle so he can represent them when he goes to Jerusalem. In this chapter, we will look at four sections of Romans in which Paul lays out the basis for having a united church, one that binds both the Jewish and the gentile believers in Christ in a common cause.

Our passages from Romans, like those from Matthew, are from the lectionary readings following Pentecost for Year A. These passages also give us important perspectives to consider as we think about the church's engagement with social issues.

As we look at these passages, it will be helpful to note that Paul writes after having taken up a collection from the predominantly gentile churches that he has founded to give to the poor members of the church in Jerusalem. He sees this collection as a way to try to hold together two quite different ways of living the faith. The church in Jerusalem was almost entirely made up of Jewish members. They remained faithful Jews who kept the law as other Jews did. The churches Paul founded were made up mostly of non-Jews who did not keep those aspects of the law that made Jews stand out from others (for example, keeping the Sabbath and the Mosaic food laws). Writing as the apostle of the gentiles, Paul wants this collection to show how the mostly gentile churches recognize their debt to those Jewish church members who were the first to believe in Christ. Since the church in Rome had more gentiles than Jews, Paul wanted them to be included among the churches he represented in Jerusalem. So, he sets out his gospel, his teaching about the way that Christ's life, death, and resurrection bring salvation, in a way that he hopes will lead the Roman church to accept him as their apostle.

Romans 1:18–5:11

At the beginning of the main part of the letter, Paul introduces himself to the Romans with a lengthy discussion of why people need the salvation that his gospel about Christ brings and of how this gospel fills the need he identifies. In

1:18–5:11 he says that people need the gospel because they are guilty. He talks about sin as acts that make people guilty before God. The solution to this problem is that the work of Christ allows God to forgive those sins and remain just. But that is only one way to think about why people need the gospel.

Romans 5:12–7:6

Paul offers another analysis in 5:12–7:6. In this section, he talks about Sin as a power that captures and enslaves all people. Sin is here pictured as a personal force that actively works in the world. We sometimes talk about Satan as a power that opposes God. Paul makes Sin that kind of power that has an active will. This power forces those it enslaves, which is everyone, to do bad things, to sin, and act against the will of God. From this perspective, what people need is not forgiveness, but rescue. Paul, then, describes the work of Christ as the thing that pulls believers out of the power of Sin and makes them God's possession. Rather than being "slaves of Sin," they become God's slaves. Being brought into God's household means that they are given eternal life instead of the certain death that awaited us all when Sin owned us.

In this passage, Paul uses language that troubles us. He talks about us being slaves either to sin or to God. We might rather think in terms of whose team we are on. After all, then we could still identify with our teammates or other fans and work for common goals. But the imagery of slavery is not accidental here. Paul knows that being enslaved entails great horrors. But it is a metaphor that emphasizes the completeness of being owned by Sin that he sees in the world. He also knows that people cannot free themselves. They must be rescued. Once they are taken into the household of God and given the blessings this includes, the metaphor of slavery also denotes that they must completely dedicate themselves to the will of God. As people who have been rescued and given new life, giving back all that believers are is the only proper response.

Seeing Sin as an enslaving power expands and challenges how we think about sin. We don't usually think of sin as a power that can force us to live in a certain way. We are pretty sure we are free to do as we please. We believe in the power of the individual. We are sure we are not owned by anyone; we are not slaves to anything or anybody. Perhaps. But what Paul says here seems to express a truth we cannot escape.

If we think in terms broader than sin as some bad deed I might do, there is a sense in which we are trapped in sin and are constantly forced to violate God's will. This predicament is sometimes talked about as living with systemic sin. When we reflect on it for a moment, we can recognize that the cultural, economic, and social systems of the world do not operate according to the will of God. They do not provide justice and mercy to all people.

Yes, there are moments when we actively acknowledge that this is the case and perhaps protest against it in some way, but most of the time we live in it without being conscious of it. That is the case because we are those who benefit from the injustice rather than those who are harmed by it. But there are large groups of our fellow citizens for whom the sinfulness of these systems is a constant oppressor. Think about going to the grocery store, for example. Much, probably most, of what you see there was harvested or packed or processed by people who work under conditions and for wages that are below what most of us would accept for ourselves or our children. Migrant farm workers are not paid a wage that allows them to have decent housing, certainly not housing we would find acceptable for ourselves. Maybe we can buy fair trade coffee or tea, but often other kinds of alternatives are not available.

Even if we could get all of our food from vendors who treat workers justly, the problem does not stop there. The same kinds of injustices are part of the manufacture of the clothes we wear, the cars we drive, the phones we use. Those products or some parts of them are produced in dangerous conditions, sometimes by children, and by people who are paid so little they remain permanently in poverty. This doesn't just happen to people in other parts of the world. There are systems that harm our neighbors at home as well—dangerous conditions for factory workers and truck drivers, exploitive labor practices and hourly wage structures that hold people in poverty. For example, think of the many people who work for minimum wage, a minimum wage that often does not bring workers up to what our government recognizes as a livable wage.

But all people must eat, and we must have clothes. We are trapped by and required to participate in and support economic systems that perpetuate injustice. By participating in these systems we harm those people who have to labor under unfair conditions—and we cannot stop participating in this way. This is, at least in part, what Paul is talking about in Romans 6 when he says that we are trapped by Sin and forced to do things that violate God's will.

Maybe we could go off and live like hermits and just eat off the land. Then we wouldn't be hurting other people. But that is no real solution. If we separate ourselves from everyone and everything to avoid doing harm, we also can't do any good that might change things. Besides, historically most hermits didn't completely escape the system because they relied on people bringing them things to wear or to eat.

Romans 6:12–23

Fortunately, Paul does not leave us in complete despair. He also declares that Christians have been set free from Sin and now serve a new master. He makes it sound like the transfer of ownership is complete. If so, it would seem to mean that believers would be able to stop contributing to the oppression of those at the bottom of the economic ladder. But Paul knows that believers must still live in a world that is ruled by Sin. Because this is the case, they cannot escape all its harm or completely escape contributing to the continuing dominance of Sin. This is similar to Paul's description of salvation. In the present, Christians have the beginning of their experience of salvation with a taste of the goodness God has in store for them, but they don't have the fullness of salvation in this life. The experience of the presence of God they have now is the guarantee that God will give them the fullness of salvation at the proper time. But their experience of salvation is partial now, just as freedom from Sin is partial in the present.

Since God now owns Christians and has brought them into the goodness of life in God's household, they are encouraged to live as God wants them to live. Because Sin is no longer their owner, Paul says they must not allow it to rule their lives. They must constantly be on the alert because Sin wants to kidnap them again. Part of their freedom from Sin is that they can see past the lies Sin tells about what is important and what gives meaning to life. This makes them free to pursue those things that bring real peace and goodness. But Paul has to tell the Romans they must not let the power of Sin lure them back into serving the purposes of evil. Instead he says they are to present their bodies as "instruments of righteousness" (6:13). That is not an easy task. Paul's reminders make that perfectly clear. Believers are called to make such decisions every day, every moment.

Paul is not just calling individuals to personal morality. Remember, this chapter of Romans is not primarily about the individual sins people commit. It is about how the world and its systems are captured by the power of Sin. It is in the context of a Sin-ruled world that Paul tells the Roman church members to be instruments of righteousness. It is in the Sin-ruled world that he calls the Romans to stop being used by Sin and to start producing goodness. Just as Sin is not only about individual acts that make us guilty, so this righteousness is not just pious living of a personal moral code. This righteousness includes seeking God's will in the world, as well as in one's own heart. It must work to promote God's will in the Sin-ruled social and economic systems of the world.

The new identity God gives believers in Christ demands that they be engaged in trying to make the systems we live in more like God wants them to be. Paul says believers are made slaves of God. This means they are required to do what God wants. Among the things God wants is a world in which all people are valued and the values of justice and mercy rule. Working for this kind of world is what God expects of God's servants. In this context, such work is what it means to work toward sanctification (6:19), that is, having the kind of life that reflects God's holiness. Working to make the lives of others better by opposing the injustices in our social, political, economic, and cultural systems is one way Christians live out the life God gives them in Christ. It is one way they share that life with others. Their lives and how they use their influence to shape cultural and governmental structures will either contribute to the spread of God's will for the world or support the unjust systems.

Romans 7:15–25a

We have seen Paul explain why we need the gospel that proclaims the salvation believers receive from Christ in two ways: we do things that make us guilty and we are forced to sin because we must live by the rules of our economic and social systems. As if those were not bad enough, he is going to explore the pernicious nature of sin from one more angle. In 7:7–8:39, Paul describes sin as something that lives within us. Sin is not just out there luring us to do wrong and enslaving us, it is within us urging us to do things we know are wrong. And we can't resist. Again, this seems like a hopeless plight. But we know there is an important truth here too. We know that nothing makes something more desirable than being told you can't have it. It doesn't matter if it's a piece of cake or a house in a more expensive subdivision. Tell me I can't have it and I want it all the more. Paul says this is what the sin that lives in us does to us.

But, again, Paul does not leave us in that sad state. He says that God rescues believers from this too. Through Christ, God sends the Spirit to live in believers and to strengthen them. He says that the intimate presence of God in believers strengthens them to live more like what God wants for us. As with other blessings that come through the work of Christ, they do not yet have this blessing in its fullness. They have the Spirit, but they do not yet live in the full presence of God. In the present, both sin and the Spirit are in believers. Since the Spirit is in them, they are better able to resist the pull of sin to do what they know is wrong, but they still struggle to discern God's will and then they struggle to do it.

It is important to recognize that Paul is saying that the sin that lives in us can keep us from discerning correctly what God's will is. We saw in chapter 1 that many in the church see government policies as a last resort for helping people who are disadvantaged, poor, and marginalized. If we were to ask them or members of our own congregations who lean in that direction whether God wants us to help the needy or make sure that all children are safe and have sufficient provisions, the vast majority would say "of course!" But our choices are not as simple as deciding whether to help those who have needs or not. If we take seriously what Paul says about sin, we will recognize that our attempts to discern how and when to help are always tainted by sin.

All of our policy decisions and political philosophies divert from what God wants because of the sin that lives in each of us. No political system or ideology has perfected policies that offer aid while also assuring and building the full dignity of all people involved. The good that we want to do is always tainted by the sin within us. One of the primary manifestations of that sin within is self-interest. Whatever good we look to do, self-interest diverts us from fully discerning what needs to be done. Even if we have the ideal of creating a just society, self-interest keeps us from discerning what it looks like, much less implementing it. It seems fairly clear that taming self-interest is not even a goal or a value for some who claim to follow the one who gave his life for them. Sin within us can even keep us from seeing how privileging self-interest contradicts any claim that we are imitating Jesus.

Our text says that sin has a way of getting us to do things that we know are opposed to God's will. That sin within us is good at coming up with reasons to justify the choices it leads us to. As it lives within us, it is one of those "voices of reason" that can lead us to accept, even work for, policies and structures that ignore the needs of others and promote our own good. After all, we work hard for what we have, right? Others should have the drive to make their own way, shouldn't they? When we hear these voices, we have to remember that sin already controls the systems. As Paul said in Romans 6, they are not just. This individualistic outlook is one of the prominent manifestations of that sin within us, especially the sin of privileging self-interest. Paul says there is a war going on within our very selves. It is a constant struggle to hold self-interest, among other sins, at bay.

This sin within us knows how to take advantage of our fears and insecurities. It can lead us from the shock and fear that terrorist acts evoke to the prejudice that leads to refusing to see the image of God in people who belong to the religious or ethnic groups those terrorists come from. Only sin could move us from mourning over senseless violence and the killing of innocent people in our group or nation to refusing to help hungry and poorly housed children "of them" in refugee camps. Only sin could convince good people that it is a good idea to cut funding for feeding hungry children because their parents are irresponsible or addicted. Only sin could convince us that we should lower taxes for wealthy people because they have worked hard, while we reduce help for God's children who live in conditions that we know are demeaning.

But we can remember that Paul does not leave us in complete despair. This analysis of the sin within us is followed by the promise that there is no condemnation in Christ and that the Spirit sets believers free from the shackles of sin. We never completely overcome this sin that is within, but we are enabled to act as God's people; we are enabled to live for God and work for the justice and mercy God wants for the world.

As Paul looks at how things are in the world, he won't allow our comfortable adages and excuses. It's not enough to say that if the church would do what it should, there would be no need for government intervention. That rings too false as we look at the size and non-action of the church. Paul would not allow the comforting assertion that we all want what's best for others, we just think there are different ways to do it. He knows the sin that lies within moves us to put self-interest above the common good and to put what is best for me above the good of the people who are economically and socially vulnerable. The sin that dwells within grows stronger when we feel threatened, whether that threat is physical or a threat to our economic and social privilege and advantage. It can even lead us to believe that we are being treated unjustly when someone tries to level the playing field or give some advantages to people who are poor or who have been disadvantaged by the way the system has worked in the past. Some in our churches, and certainly in the church across the country, have supported policies and programs that play into their own self-interests rather than the interests of those who need help or who have been harmed by unjust systems. When they do, they are fighting the same battle we all face. It is the battle between what God wants and the sin that lies within.

As we fight this battle, some of us seem to gain or lose ground in the battle against the sin within in some areas; some of us gain or lose ground in others. Sin will have the power to keep all of us from discerning with complete clarity what God's will is for different moral, economic, and social issues. When some of us are blinded by the sin within to support policies that feed self-interest, others must show love by pointing to God's fuller will. God's will must not be identified with any political party. No political party or its platform has ever rid itself of self-interest to an extent that would allow us to say that it fully reflects God's justice, love, and mercy. The power of that sin within us constantly diverts us, as individuals and churches and as social and political groups, from God's full will. The church must be in the business of constantly discerning God's will and exposing the work of sin that so easily turns us from it. The church should be in the business of helping its members discern which policies point more toward God's fuller will and which ones point away from it.

We should remember, too, that sin does not have the last word. God has sent the Spirit into the hearts of believers to help them discern and do God's will. We may not get it just right, but God does not abandon us in the hands of sin. With God's help we can proclaim the values of the kingdom of God as those that God wants to govern the whole earth. And we can work to make them the values that guide our own governments.

Appendix on Romans 13:1–7

As we noted in chapter 1, some interpreters look to Romans 13:1–7 to argue that the functions of government should be limited to maintaining order. But if we read this text carefully, we see that it is not prescribing what government should be or do, but rather telling the church in Rome how they should relate to the government. This passage acknowledges some legitimate actions for governments, but does not present a comprehensive account of what they should do. Again, this passage is about how church members relate to the government, not about what the government should do.

At the same time, this passage says that the governments that exist are here because that is God's will. Paul says they exist to promote the doing of good and the punishment of those who do wrong. Some have taken this to mean that Christians should not oppose the policies of the government because they are God's will. But such an outlook had churches supporting the Nazis in the 1940s and opposing the civil rights movement in the 1950s and 60s.

When Paul says governments exist because they are God's will, he is following a line of thought that appears in the prophets of Israel. We have already seen in chapter 3 that the prophets say that God has expectations of nations and judges them when they violate God's will. We can look to other texts from the prophets to see that acknowledging that governments are set in place by God does not mean God's people should not oppose their unjust policies. The prophets of Israel and Judah are constantly opposing the policies of their kings. Jeremiah tells the king of Judah and the surrounding kingdoms that God has made Nebuchadnezzar the king of Babylon and that it is God's will that all submit to the power of the Babylonian king (Jer 27:1–7). Jeremiah can even refer to Nebuchadnezzar as a "servant of God" (25:9; 27:6). This does not mean that everything he did or every policy he had was pleasing to God or that all of God's people should blindly obey all laws. After all,

Nebuchadnezzar worshipped many gods and wanted others to do the same.

In the book of Daniel, we hear that God gave power to Nebuchadnezzar (2:37–38) and that God punished him for doing wrong (4:25). That God put him in office also did not mean Daniel always obeyed him. In the beginning of the book, Daniel and others refuse to eat things that violate their religion (1:3–21), and later Daniel directly violates the king's order and continues to pray to God (6:1–28). God seems to approve of this disobedience because God saved Daniel when he was thrown into the lion's den for it.

Paul would have assuredly told church members not to offer incense to the gods of Rome or the genius of Caesar. Those refusals were clear violations of government demands. We can be sure that in Romans 13 he is not calling for the readers to accept any and all governmental policies or demands. Like the Israelite prophets, Paul can say the government is both there by the will of God and that it does evil that God's people should resist. We might note that the only direct application of this submission to the government is that the readers should pay their taxes (13:5–7).

Paul probably encouraged believers to submit to the authority of the government because to do otherwise would attract attention to the church and increase the likelihood of persecution, both official and nonofficial. After all, Paul's readers lived in the heart of the empire. Disobedience would have been met with swift punishment that might extend to the whole church.

There is a strangeness to this advice. Paul regularly calls into question the values that govern the world outside the church. He advises his churches to live by values that violate what the structures of the social, economic, and governmental systems expect. In this chapter we have seen him say that the powers of evil control the world in a way that requires us to sin. But in this direct statement about the government, he draws on that prophetic tradition to see the Roman government as authorized by God. While he does not say it here, he would also hold to the second part of that prophetic tradition that holds governments accountable to God for how they wield the power God has given them. His own martyrdom demonstrates that he did not take this submission to include violating God's will.

As with all the texts we are looking at in this study, we must remember that Paul is addressing a specific time and place. We can draw implications for how we live as the people of God, but cannot simply apply those directions to our time. In this case, Paul is writing to people who have no chance to change the political situation. Living in a democracy is much different from living under an emperor who listens only to the wealthiest and most privileged members of society. Perhaps this passage might suggest that Christians be good citizens and accept the authority of the state when it does not violate their faith and work to change it when it does.

Questions for Discussion

1. Paul says we are forced to sin. What does this understanding of sin suggest to you about the ways we have imagined our freedom, both as individuals and as collectives of churches and nations?

2. We resist the idea that we are involved in supporting unjust systems or throw up our hands about our ability to escape them. One of the excuses we make is that those people have a better life than they would have without the unjustly low wage they get. What response might we forge that better reflects the justice that God wants for all people?

3. How might we resist and fight against those economic and social systems that require us to continue to oppress others? Think about personal, community, and broader governmental and policy steps.

4. When have you felt the sin of self-interest within you luring you to do something you knew was harmful to yourself or others? What compromises has it led to that you knew were not really what God wants for yourself or the world?

5. What are some ways that the sin of privileging self-interest has shaped our society? Our decisions about tax policy? Our decisions about programs to aid people who are poor?

6. How might remembering the sin that lies within help us discern God's will in church meetings? In decisions at work? In decisions in the voting booth?

9

The Example of Jesus and the Good of Others

Let each of you look not to your own interests, but to the interests of others. Let the same mind be in you that was in Christ Jesus.

—Philippians 2:4–5

Philippians is well known for its emphasis on joy. Paul talks more about rejoicing in this letter than in any other. He is on good terms with the Philippian church. Most of Paul's letters are written to deal with a problem, but that is less the case with this letter. Paul wrote to thank the Philippians for their support of his ministry, including some money they had just sent him while he was in prison. Despite having a good relationship with this church, Paul had heard that there was a problem. Two leaders of the church, Euodia and Syntyche, were having an argument (4:1–3). Note that these leaders are both women. This is one of the indications that people have misunderstood what Paul thinks about women as leaders in the church. Beyond being leaders in the Philippian church, Paul says these women have worked with him to spread the gospel; he calls them "fellow-workers," a designation Paul uses for people on his mission team who also preach and teach. These women, then, had been colleagues in mission with Paul.

Paul never hints at what the argument between Euodia and Syntyche is about; he just asks others to help them resolve it. The argument seems to be serious enough to have caused some problems within the church. This seems to be the reason Paul writes about how church members should relate to one another in other parts of the letter. Paul uses the example of Christ as the model for how believers should treat each other. In this chapter, we'll see if there are hints that believers should also treat those outside their church in the same way.

Giving Away the Advantage

In Philippians 2:1–5, Paul reminds this church of the love, comfort, and fellowship they have with God and calls on them to adopt a single mindset of selflessness. When he says he wants them to "be of the same mind" he doesn't mean they have to agree about everything, but that they get along with one another. He borrows this language from political speeches of that time that try to persuade the citizens of a city to get along and to adopt a way of moving forward.

In verses 3–4, he says some very radical and countercultural things. First, he tells the church to act with humility. While unity was a cultural value in the first century, humility was not. It was a culture that encouraged people to take advantage of others when they could, as a way of showing one's power and honor. It was considered shameful to be humble. It meant that someone had bested you and that brought dishonor to you. But Paul tells Jesus's followers to be humble; he tells them to reject the self-interested values of the broader society. This would not only disadvantage them socially and economically, it would lead people to think less of them.

The next command is even more extraordinary. Paul tells the Philippians to think of others as better than themselves. Paul isn't telling them to have poor self-esteem. He doesn't want them to think less of themselves, he just wants them to think more of the other person. Paul has already celebrated their generosity to him and his love for them. He has just reminded them that they are among those God is saving. So, he's clearly not trying to crush their spirits or make them devalue their own worth. He does want them to adopt a new way of looking at, relating to, and valuing others.

He tells them to make the interests of other people more important than their own interests. This is broad language that encompasses all aspects of life. Paul says they are to give preference to the welfare of fellow believers, rather than to their own. This runs counter to what they saw as the proper way of orienting one's life. Aren't we supposed to take care of our own needs and those of our family first?

Just when it sounds like Paul has gone too far, he offers an explanation of why this should be the direction of their lives in the form of an early church liturgy (vv. 6–11). Many scholars identify it as a hymn. Paul is citing it as evidence for his instruction about putting the good of others before your own good. This liturgy tells of Christ leaving heaven to come to earth and of his obedience to God's will. It says that at first, Christ had a place so high that it was not an exaggeration for him to claim equality with God. But Christ gave that up to come to earth and obey God, even to the point of being killed. It then tells of God's response to that way of living: God exalts Christ, making him ruler of the whole cosmos. Remember, Paul introduces this liturgy by calling the Philippians to adopt the same outlook that they see in Christ (v. 5).

Paul gives the Philippians a pattern to imitate. Just as Christ gave up the honors of heaven to come to earth, so they are to give up their advantages for the good of others. They have been given forgiveness and relationship with God, citizenship in the kingdom of God, and salvation through Christ, who put their good before his own. Paul is simply asking them to do for one another what Christ has already done for them. Christ's self-giving is to lead those who believe in him to being willing to give of themselves for the good of others.

God's response to Christ giving himself for the good of others is crucial. The liturgy says that God responds to this self-giving by exalting Christ to the highest position in the cosmos. Since he is in that position, every being in all of creation must submit to him. They must bow before him and confess that he is Lord. This text raises many theological questions, but we must limit ourselves to thinking about what it says about how we relate to other people in the church, and outside it.

Preference for the Affairs of Christ

When God makes Jesus Lord, Jesus is not Lord only of the church. He is Lord over all of creation and over all beings in creation. It may well be that bowing and acknowledging Jesus as Lord in this scene is not voluntary. That is, this is not a hope that all will come to love Jesus, but an assertion that all will be required to acknowledge his position, power, and rule. When Rome conquered a region, it did not ask (at least immediately) people to love it. It demanded that everyone acknowledge and submit to its rule. That is probably what the author of this liturgy was thinking of when she or he wrote those lines. All people and all governments will be required to submit to Christ and his rule.

The point of making Jesus Lord over everything is that he imposes the will of God on all things. Clearly that is not the case at the present time, but it is the promise of this text. This suggests that God is interested in the way the world and its systems work, not just in how Christians behave or how they behave toward one another. As the people who acknowledge the lordship of Christ, Christians are to work to further the realization of his will in all aspects of life. That includes the political, social, and economic systems that we live in.

When we hear Paul say we are to put the good of others ahead of our own good because that is what Christ did, we say, "Wait just a minute. Jesus was the Son of God; only he could live like that. You can't have the same expectation for us mere mortals." That is exactly what Paul expected the Philippians to say! So, he built into this letter examples of mere mortals doing just that. His first example is himself. Before he introduces this liturgy about Christ, he has already talked about how he is willing to suffer imprisonment because it has advanced the gospel and it has made others more courageous in proclaiming the message for which he has been jailed (1:12–14). His good is not as important as the advance of the gospel or the encouragement of other believers. Not only is Paul in prison, he knows there are some church members who preach to make him mad. He says that is also fine—in fact, he will be happy about it, because their work also advances the gospel (1:15–19). Finally, he says that his imprisonment and the other things he has endured in his ministry have made his life so difficult that he would be better off if he died so he could be with Christ. But he is determined to stay alive because that is what is best for the Philippians (1:21–26). In all these ways, Paul puts the good of others ahead of his own good.

Of course, we can respond by saying, "Yeah, but he was an apostle." Again, that seems to be what Paul thought the Philippians would say. He does not give them that out. After quoting the liturgy about Christ putting the good of others above his own, Paul talks about two other people who live by this example of Christ: Timothy and Epaphroditus. First, Paul tells them about Timothy, a person they know. Paul says he is about to send Timothy to visit them. He describes Timothy as someone who genuinely cares for them. Paul says everyone else puts their own affairs, their own good, first, but not Timothy. He puts the affairs of Christ above what is good for him. Paul reminds the Philippians that they have seen Timothy behave like this (2:19–24).

But again, this is someone who has this special relationship with an apostle, not a regular person. So Paul's next example of following Christ's model is a member of their own church, Epaphroditus. The Philippians had sent him to take their gift and to help Paul while he was in prison. Paul writes that Epaphroditus has done a good job serving him on the Philippians' behalf. But even more, Epaphroditus did this when he was so sick he nearly died. Paul tells the church that their friend was willing to risk his life for the work of Christ (2:25–30). Paul is clear that Christians are required to consider the needs of others more important than their own. Christ's example is meant to shape the way all Christians live and think of others.

This demand is as countercultural now as it was in the first century. We really don't believe we should put the needs of others above ours. We say things like, "You have to love yourself first to be able to love others," or "You have to have things for yourself so you can share." These have some truth to them, but they are usually excuses for rejecting this expectation of the faith. Our culture tells us we need to care for ourselves and those in our family or our group more than we care about others. We are constantly encouraged to do what is best for ourselves, even if it comes at the expense of others. We decide who belongs within the circle of those who deserve our primary concern differently at different times. Sometimes it is just our immediate family; at other times our culture has defined it as our own social class, gender, or race. The example of Christ demands that we reject those claims to hold onto our own advantage and seek to do what is good for others even when that means accepting some disadvantage.

We need to be clear about the meaning of this expectation that Christians will follow Christ's example in putting the good of others first. When this expectation has been encouraged, it has often been used to do great harm. It has been used to tell women they should stay in abusive relationships because that is following this command. People who have been treated unjustly because of their ethnicity or their economic status have been told they should endure it because Christ accepted suffering. These are tragic misuses of this demand. Note that the people who give up something in each of these examples from Philippians have more power than the ones they defer to. Christ had great power that he gave up for the sake of those who had need.

Paul was the apostle with the authority to bring good news to the Philippians, but he used that authority to accept disadvantage and suffering to help the Philippians who needed the gospel.

Timothy was an associate of the apostle, and Epaphroditus was a person with significant status in the church. Both accepted disadvantage for the good of those with less power and status. That is the pattern of this example. Whenever following Christ's example is used to tell the disadvantaged person or the person who has less power to suffer for the one with more power, this command is being misused.

Those misuses do not, however, allow the church to ignore the demand that people with more power and status make the good of those with less status more important than their own. If the church takes seriously the call to put the good of others ahead of our own, it will reshape how we relate to one another and our discussions about what our churches should do to work for justice. When we remember that the liturgy in Philippians 2 makes Christ the ruler of all things, not just the church, it becomes clear that the command to adopt the mindset of Christ means that the church should work for social and economic policies that give advantages to those who are poor and disadvantaged.

This seems to violate our ideas about how to act and organize life just as much as it did for the Philippians. We might claim that things need to be fair, that everyone should get the same treatment. But that's not what this passage calls for. The way to follow the example of Christ is not to be fair in the sense that we make sure every person gives or gets the same amount. The way to imitate Christ is to give others the advantage. This means Christians will have to give up resources and power they could have had in order to do what is good for others. It means Christians will have to support policies that help others even when those policies and laws bring disadvantages to them. Christians can act this way because God has already shown this kind of love to us and given us gifts that are far greater than anything we could give. Christians can follow Christ's example because we know what God's reaction to such self-giving is. God responded to Christ's self-giving by exalting him to the highest position possible. Similarly, God will respond to Christians' willingness to put others first by bringing us into God's own presence and giving us the fullest life with God.

Questions for Discussion

1. We don't expect our Christian values to contradict our cultural values, but putting the good of others above our own does. How can we shape our churches in such a way that shows that we think about living by what God expects rather than conforming to the values and expectations of our culture?

2. How do you react to the expectation that Christians should put the good of others above their own good? Do you find it as difficult as Paul thinks the Philippians will find it? How can we balance this command with the need to care for our own families?

3. What would change in your community if your church began to live out the command to put the good of others above our own good in its outreach in the community? How might this command shape your church's budgets and agendas?

4. Philippians says God has made Christ the ruler of all things, not just the church. What might that suggest about how the church follows his example of accepting disadvantage for the good of others in its participation in discussions of social and economic policies and laws? About immigration policies? About healthcare policies?

5. Given that Christ is ruler of all things, how might the church follow his example of giving advantages to people who are poor? How, for example, might that influence our discussions of tax policy? Who would the policy give advantages to? Who would it disadvantage? What might the church say about cutting aid to people who are experiencing poverty in order to lower the taxes of those who have more?

10

Revelation on World Governments

Jesus Christ, faithful witness, firstborn from the dead, and
ruler of the kings of the earth
—Revelation 1:5

It might seem odd to include the book of Revelation in a discussion about the church's role in shaping social and economic policy, but John, the author of the book, has a lot to say about what God expects of governments. Revelation may be the New Testament book that most consistently expresses opposition to the Roman Empire. Of course, it veils its criticism in symbolic language, but Revelation paints Rome as a primary manifestation of evil in the world. It's given that role not only because of the way it treats church members, but also because of its oppressive economic policies and the violence it uses to expand and hold power.

Still, a central reason Rome is singled out as a primary

manifestation of evil is that it supports and carries out persecution of the church. All of the churches John was writing to had experienced some kind of persecution, and John himself was in exile at the time, sent to the island of Patmos off the coast of Turkey. Roman persecution of the church was sporadic, but the persecution by local officials who represented Rome could be more persistent. Much of this persecution was social and economic, but there had also been some executions. By the time Revelation was written, both Paul and Peter had already been executed. Nero had already executed many believers in Rome. John mentions martyrs in the cities he's writing to (2:13; 6:9–11). Even if the persecution was not so overt in a particular city, knowing that the power of the empire could easily be unleashed against the church made all church members feel vulnerable. It is easy to see why John sees the Roman government as the embodiment of evil.

A Grim Vision

The first sign that John has the conduct of nations in view comes at the very beginning of the book, in 1:5. Here he calls Christ, among other things, "the ruler of the kings of the earth." So, all kings are answerable to him for the ways they rule. John's readers would have understood this because Rome gave people the title of "king" and then expected them to rule the way they wanted them to rule. This title for Christ suggests, then, that all kings, and so all governments, are to govern in ways that conform to Christ's will. John follows this by saying that Christ has made believers a kingdom (v. 6). That is, the primary identity of believers is a citizenship that is different from Roman citizenship or any other citizenship or allegiance. Their citizenship in Christ's kingdom must take precedence over all other citizenships and loyalties.

The rest of chapters 1–3 has Christ dictating letters to seven churches in what is now western Turkey. These letters tell them how they need to change so they are more pleasing to Christ. Then, chapters 4–5 contain visions of heaven, with chapter 4 focusing on the worship of God and chapter 5 on the worship of Christ. The last part of chapter 5 introduces a scroll that seems to tell of how God will act in response to the persecution the church is experiencing. But the scroll is locked with seven seals that no one can open, no one except Christ.

The action of the book starts as Christ opens the first seal at the beginning of chapter 6. As each seal is removed, we see a kind of judgment against those who oppose God's will. Each of the first four of these seals releases one of the famous Four Horsemen of the Apocalypse. They are not as mysterious as we sometimes think. The first two bring war: John says the first goes out conquering and the next takes peace from the earth with a big sword. We need to remember that all the images in Revelation are symbolic. John does not think that a literal red horse is going to show up some day. Rather, this is John's way of talking about things that are happening in his world. As he thinks of the wars among nations, and particularly those that Rome engages, he sees them as a judgment from God. Rulers and nations start wars to benefit themselves, but John sees having the wars as a manifestation of God's judgment. The next two horsemen bring what happens in the aftermath of war. First, food prices skyrocket, and a famine follows. All we have to do is think of all the refugee camps that spring up wherever there is a war to know that John has perceived accurately at least some of the evil consequences of war.

The seal that follows the horses changes the scene so that we see martyrs asking God how long it will be before God avenges their deaths (6:9–11). These martyrs were killed, of course, by the Roman Empire. To ask when God will do justice for them is to ask when God will put an end to Rome and its unjust violence against the innocent.

There are many books written in the literary style of Revelation, and the cosmic calamities of the sixth seal (the sun goes black and the moon becomes blood) are traditional images in writings like Revelation. John and the churches he writes to know these works and so are able to understand the imagery more readily than we are. They know that such actions symbolize that the ultimate judgment is about to take place. What's notable here is who John says is frightened by the coming judgment. His list has kings, people of high status, high-ranking military officers, the rich, the powerful, and then everyone else (6:15–16). John seems to be indicating that those who are powerful and wealthy should be particularly worried about the coming judgment. He is saying at the least that their money and power will not exempt them from judgment. Those who should have been making the social, political, and economic systems of the world conform to God's will are singled out for special mention as those who should fear the coming judgment.

A First Glimpse at God's Reign

The plot in Revelation is not linear but cyclical, as John returns to images of the judgment of God that can be seen in the world in the present. The opening of the final seal on the scroll doesn't bring the end of the world. Instead, it introduces a new set of instruments to keep the action moving: seven trumpets. The final trumpet introduces the first climactic section in Revelation, 11:15–19. This section has been made famous by the inclusion of its opening in the Hallelujah chorus in Handel's *Messiah*. Judgment day begins in this scene with God taking over as king of all the earth. "The kingdom of the world has become the kingdom of our Lord and of his Messiah" (11:15). Now, finally, things will conform to God's will. John is concerned about more than the conduct of individuals here. Remember that he has had his eye on Rome's conduct from the beginning. In 11:18, John says that "the nations" are angry because God is now imposing God's will on the earth. Justice is now done for all the faithful and condemnation comes to those who "destroy the earth." This comment is not primarily about ecology, but that is included. This is more centrally about those people and governments who have done all kinds of damage to the world through injustice and violence, the things John has been talking about since chapter 6.

John's use of such extravagant imagery and symbolism often makes it hard for us to understand the kinds of conduct he wants to single out as evil or who he has in mind as those who are doing evil. We have to remind ourselves that John expects his original readers to understand the symbols he uses much more easily than we understand them. Again, those churches were used to reading this kind of material, so they know what the symbols mean. John occasionally steps outside the usual repertoire of imagery and so must explain what he means. That is what he does in chapters 17–18.

Babylon the Great

Chapter 17 begins with perhaps the most horrific and offensive image of the whole book. John says he is shown a giant prostitute who sits on many waters. He is told that she has committed adultery with the kings of the earth and that the inhabitants of the earth were drunk on the wine of her sexual immorality. Then he sees her sitting on a scarlet beast that has seven heads and ten horns with blasphemous names all over it. The woman is dressed in purple and scarlet, wearing a gold crown that has all sorts of precious jewels, and she is holding a cup that is full of defiling things. Her name is tattooed on her forehead: Babylon the great, mother of prostitutes and abominations. As she sits on the beast she is drunk on the blood of martyrs. After this horrifying description, John writes, "I was greatly amazed." And rightly so!

This image is so strange that John does not think his readers will automatically know what it means. So, an angel explains just enough of it to make sure John and his readers understand. At 17:9 the angel says, "This calls for a mind that has wisdom." In Revelation, that sentence means that an explanation is coming. Then he says the seven heads of the beast are seven hills that the woman sits on. This may not help us much, but it is all that John's readers need for them to know what is being depicted. As is the case today, many ancient cities had nicknames. Those we know today include "The Big Apple" for New York and "Tinsel Town" for Hollywood. In the first century, the nickname for Rome was "The City of Seven Hills." So when John says that the woman is seated on seven hills, everyone knows he is talking about Rome. This woman is John's image of the Roman Empire.

John's comments about the woman's sexual immorality probably draw on the Hebrew prophets who used that metaphor to refer to Israel worshipping other gods. John seems to identify idolatry as a major sin of Rome because of the emperor cult. Adding one more sacrifice was not a problem for anyone other than Jews and members of the church. Offering incense to the emperor showed loyalty to the empire. Few people would have seen it as much of an imposition because they already worshipped many gods. But for Jews and members of the church, it was a violation of the command to worship only God, a command no one else thought about. By the time Revelation is written, church members had been martyred for not being willing to offer incense to the genius of the emperor. That's the reason John says the woman is drunk on the blood of martyrs.

But that's not her only sin. Her extraordinarily opulent dress also points to her greed as a central sin. So does her gold crown that is decorated with jewels. John further identifies her with what Jewish readers would see as the ultimate evil empire, Babylon. It was the Babylonian empire that sacked Jerusalem and exiled its residents in the sixth century B.C.E. Since that time, Babylon had been the symbol of evil, especially an evil government that imposes its will on God's people. By identifying Rome with Babylon, John makes Rome the archenemy of God and the people of God.

John's further discussion of this woman and the beast she rides tells of how rulers and kings have given power to her and of how she opposes the will of God and the people of God. The whole world, he says, has come under her power. Just so his readers remember that he is talking about Rome, at the end of his description he says the woman is "the great city that rules over the kings of the earth" (v. 18). Notice how this description of her rule is a challenge to the description of Christ as the "ruler of the kings of the earth" that we saw above (1:5).

At the beginning of chapter 18, an angel declares that

Babylon has fallen. So, John looks into the future when God defeats the empire. Rome is destroyed because of the sin it committed and promoted. John singles out kings and merchants of luxury goods as those who are especially complicit in Rome's sin (18:3). After warnings against participating in Rome's culture, we hear a series of dirges from those who profited from the evil of Rome. These come from kings who "lived in luxury with her" (18:9–10), merchants of luxury goods (18:11–17), and ship captains (18:17–19). All of these wealthy and powerful people mourn the loss of the evil empire because they profited from its injustice. And all of them share its condemnation. Rome is said to be a deserted city because its powerful merchants deceived the people (18:23–24).

This extensive scene shows us what John sees as the central sins that lead to God's judgment on Rome: killing martyrs, demanding that all participate in the emperor cult, violence-enforced dominance of other nations, and an unjust economic structure. It was an economic system that helped some people become very wealthy and powerful, in large measure by treating those below them unjustly. When we think about how God evaluates governments, John would make sure we see that unjust economic systems are among the things God condemns. Clearly John is not talking here about how God judges within the church. He sees God concerned with what governments require of their residents and what economic system they set in place. Since God is concerned about national economic systems, it seems reasonable that Christ's church should be active in trying to shape economic policy.

Systems of Justice and Mercy

We have seen that throughout Revelation, God is interested in the conduct of nations, not just the conduct of the church and not just the conduct of individuals. Revelation shows us a God who is concerned about the social and economic policies of nations. A social policy that encourages people to honor anyone or anything above God is explicitly condemned. So are economic policies that enrich the few who deal with those who are wealthy and powerful. John was in no position to work for change in the empire's policies and laws, but he was clear about what God thinks of systems that do not conform to God's justice and mercy. Governments are responsible for having policies that conform to God's will.

Seeing that God expects certain behavior from nations implies that Christians should be working to shape the national policies of their nations so that they conform to God's will. In Revelation, God is concerned about foreign policy, as well as the persecution of the church. God condemns foreign policy that imposes dominance through violence and war. We see in Revelation that God is concerned about economic policy, as well as the worship of other gods. Economic systems that enrich the people who are already wealthy and powerful bring God's judgment. In Revelation's judgment scenes, John emphasizes the place of political leaders and those who are wealthy and powerful in receiving condemnation, but all who cooperate in these unjust systems are also condemned. This again indicates that God's people should be active in working to shape governmental policies and systems so they move toward conforming to God's will. John does not describe what kinds of governmental policies would be pleasing to God, but as we have seen, he does tell us of things that are unacceptable. The other biblical texts we have looked at do point us to what God wants in such policies. At the least, God demands policies that reflect God's own justice and mercy. We will think more about what these demands mean for the church today in our final chapter.

Questions for Discussion

1. It might be surprising to see how much focus there is on the Roman Empire in Revelation, rather than solely on the church. What might this say about the role of the church in shaping national social and economic policies?

2. John's grotesque description of the woman who represents the Roman Empire includes presenting her dressed in very expensive clothes and having extraordinarily expensive jewelry (her crown). How does this fit with the way we've seen other parts of the Bible talk about the ways economic systems should work? What might this suggest about a government that has policies that promote the accumulation of wealth for its leaders, those close to them, and those already wealthy? What might this say about inheritance laws and taxes on large inheritances?

3. When John lists the luxury goods the wealthy merchants sell, he includes slaves among their wares, and then interjects that these slaves are human beings (18:11–13). Why do you think John included slaves and said this about them at the climax of this list? What might including them suggest about

God's concern about the social policies of nations and for the people harmed by social policies?

4. John tells the churches that God will overturn the injustices done by Rome and other rulers. He says God will punish rulers and those who support them for governing with unjust laws. What does this suggest about God's concern for national economic and social policies? Does it suggest anything about the church's involvement in crafting and supporting such policies? Does it suggest anything about what issues Christians should make their priorities when they vote?

5. John's message also has God's judgment come on Rome for its violence in wars and in suppressing those it conquered. What might this say about what God would want to see in policies involving international relations? What kinds of violence other than war might some kinds of international relations policies promote or restrain?

11

Being a Faithful Church
in Today's World

God is king over all the nations. —Psalm 47:8

Say among the nations, "The Lord is king." —Psalm 96:10

We have now walked through many parts of the Bible, observing what God expects from governments and authorities. In this final chapter, we will take stock of what we have seen and think about what these texts suggest about the church's participation in the political process and what kinds of policies God calls it to support. In doing so, I will offer a biblical framework for determining what that participation might look like for us and our church communities.

Protect the People Who Are Vulnerable

We saw that the Mosaic covenant included religious expectations, personal moral demands, and instructions about how to construct economic and legal systems. Most importantly, we saw that it gave special protections to those who are poor and vulnerable. It singled out immigrants as people who must be accorded the same justice that is given to citizens. This covenant required the banking system to give advantages to those who are poor, advantages that included not charging them interest and not keeping their collateral. It was not possible to separate religious life from civil and economic law. The covenant with God encompasses all aspects of life. The image of God as ruler makes it particularly clear that the laws of the covenant are to be the law of the land.

As we think about these laws, they should certainly have an influence on our economic and immigration laws. Were we to make banking laws conform to the standards of the Mosaic covenant, we would immediately outlaw payday lenders. Laws in most states allow them to charge those who are poor far more than any legal interest rate. Rather than protecting poor people, current laws allow greater exploitation of them. But drawing banking regulations closer to what the covenant demands would require much more structural change. As we noted in chapter 2, most banks charge those with lower income and less property higher interest rates. The more you qualify to borrow, the lower the interest rate. Though not as dramatically unfair as payday lending, this system still violates how God tells Israel to set up its economic system.

We cannot plead that such things may have worked for an ancient economy, but not a modern one. We must remember that when Leviticus and other books give a law, they often support it by saying that the character of God is what demands it: "You are to be holy because I am holy." It is the justice and the mercy of God that demand more just and merciful economic laws. This is not to say that the twenty-first-century legal code should look like that of ancient Israel. But the church should be using its influence to shape policies and legal systems so that they conform to the character of God, just as those ancient laws tried to do.

We learn from the Law that God is concerned about more than religious practices. God is concerned about economic laws, and God expects God's people to structure such laws so that they reflect the justice and mercy of God. This requires the church to work for laws and systems that privilege those who are poor over maximizing shareholder profits.

Starting with this Mosaic law, the biblical witness calls Christians to help shape economic systems that work for the good of all. What might that look like in your particular context? Perhaps it means lobbying to change predatory lending practices or giving incentives to banks to make loans to those who require immediate help, such as an unexpected healthcare crisis. Perhaps it means providing educational programs to help people set up bank accounts and manage their money. Make yourself aware of the economic inequities in your community and seek just solutions.

Similarly, the Mosaic law also required special treatment for immigrants and other vulnerable members of society (widows and orphans). It demanded that they not be oppressed or deprived of the rights and protections of the citizen and the privileged. As it does for the economic system, this shows that God expects civil law to extend its protections to those who are disadvantaged socially and economically. These laws are also based on who God is and how God has acted to save God's people from oppression. Having experienced the love and mercy of God who freed Israel from oppression, the Israelites were to extend the same mercy to others who are oppressed. The vulnerability of the immigrant and others without full legal protections was more important than their legal status. This suggests that God's people today should think of the treatment of immigrants and other vulnerable persons through the same lens of God's mercy and love. People of faith are called to reach out with mercy to immigrants and vulnerable people, so they can experience the justice, mercy, and goodness of God. Policies that limit help to those fleeing violence in another country violates the spirit of the Mosaic covenant and the character of God.

Churches can do much to shape the laws that govern immigration policy and the treatment of immigrant neighbors. Begin by becoming more familiar with immigration laws and programs. Support those programs that are helping to create just immigration policy. Be aware of those neighbors in your midst who are new to this country and your community. Imagine ways to welcome them and help them participate fully in society. Work with other churches to support legal and economic aid for the people who are most vulnerable among us. We can also urge lawmakers to enact more just immigration laws, and support those who do.

Seek a Just Government

The message we heard from the prophets mirrors, for the most part, what we heard in the Law of Moses. The prophets called on rulers of Israel to create just economic and social systems. The Hebrew prophets were constantly seen talking to kings and others who set social and economic policies. Those in power are to enact and enforce laws that protect those who are poor and vulnerable, but the prophets often accuse those in power when people who are poor are unjustly treated. The message of the prophets is clear: Governments and rulers are expected to enact laws and establish institutions that protect people who have fewer resources and less power.

Since these prophets most often speak to rulers who are members of the Mosaic covenant, some might say that these expectations are only for those in that covenant. But we also saw that these prophets speak to and about other nations. Nations that inflict violence on others or who commit "wickedness" (as in the case of Nineveh) also come under God's judgment. These indictments show that God expects all nations to make their laws and policies conform to God's will and character. According to these prophets, the laws of all nations are to express God's justice and mercy. What God expected of Israel is the pattern for how all nations should develop their governmental policies and laws.

God expects our laws to protect the same kinds of people and to demand justice for all. It is the church's job to discern for itself and then to help the government discern what the will of God is for all kinds of legislation. The constant orientation of both the Law and the prophets is that social and economic law is to favor people who are poor and vulnerable. Extending more of God's bounty to them is in line with God's justice.

When the church takes seriously the example of the Hebrew prophets, it will see that speaking to and trying to influence people in political office is part of its members' job as the people of God. Separation of church and state does not mean that the church ignores the injustices that our laws allow or prescribe. Churches that take the prophets seriously will allow, even embolden, their leaders to take political stands when the treatment of people who are vulnerable is at issue. They can have leaders write editorials and make other public statements in the name of the church. At the same time, churches can organize letter-writing campaigns, and those who are close enough to seats of government (county seats, state capitals, or Washington, DC) can make sure that the voices of the faithful are heard clearly.

Just Cultural Values

Our look at New Testament texts also indicates that the church should work to help the nation shape its laws to conform to God's will. We saw the earliest church rejecting the economic and social systems of the Roman world in which they lived. Wealthy church members shared their livelihoods so that the people who were poor among them could be supplied with what they needed. While this change happened only within the church, it is a demonstration of what God wants for the whole world. As Israel was to be a light to the rest of the nations, showing what God wants everywhere, so also the church that rejects the economic values of its culture is a sign to its own nation about how God expects economic and social systems to work.

Churches can organize community forums and discussion groups to examine laws and the structures that favor the rich and disadvantage people who are poor. Churches can press candidates and elected officials to take more account of the needs of those who cannot make campaign contributions. While we may not want churches to endorse candidates, we should want them to speak out when candidates support policies that move further from God's will rather than toward it. We should clearly state that our cultural individualism has led us to give advantages to those who need it the least. The early church did not simply help only those who could "pull themselves up by their own bootstraps"; they helped all in their community who had need.

Called to Meet the Needs of the Whole Person

Matthew showed us a mission of Jesus and of his disciples that was deeply concerned with the entire lives of people, not just their religious lives. The first mission of the apostles was to care for the physical needs of those who suffered physical pain or mental and spiritual pain caused by demon possession. This mission of the apostles suggests that it is part of the mission of the church to strive to make the world what God wants it to be. God's mercy and justice are not limited to charitable giving, but seek also the physical and mental well-being of the whole person.

We also found Jesus telling his disciples that being faithful to him will mean coming into conflict with the values and structures of the society that surrounds them. The parable of the Wheat and the Weeds says that the struggle against evil will be constant. The church will always be engaged in trying to grow what is good while it battles evil. The parable of the Last Judgment shows what kinds of expectations God has for people outside the church. The gentiles or "the nations" are judged according to how they treated persecuted church members. Those who are condemned ignored the physical needs of God's people who are in need. While not mentioned in the parable, we know that responding appropriately to the needs of people in distress includes more than meeting that immediate need. Any full response will include changing the governmental, social, and legal systems that impose or allow that need to arise or remain a constant in the lives of the suffering people.

If any doubt remains about whether the church's mission includes shaping the economic, social, and political laws and systems of the nations, we can turn to the Lord's Prayer. Jesus's teaching about prayer includes the request that God's will be done on earth just as it is in heaven. This is certainly not a prayer about having God's will be done only in the church. This is a prayer for God's will to be what governs all things in the world. While this is a petition addressed to God, there can be no doubt that praying this includes the expectation that God's people will be working for what God wants for the world. It would be quite hypocritical to ask God to do something that we are not willing to work toward ourselves. Matthew's Jesus says clearly that the church should want God's will to govern everything in the world.

For a church in a democracy, that means voting for candidates who support laws and policies that will reflect God's justice and mercy in shaping those policies and laws. It will mean supporting candidates who work to enact laws that privilege people who are poor and vulnerable. There may be differences of opinion about how such things should be done, but the church can work to discern which policies move us closer to or farther from God's will being done "on earth as it is in heaven."

Act as Citizens of the Kingdom

Luke gives even more attention than the other Gospels to people experiencing poverty and to those considered outcasts or second-class citizens. Luke's Jesus gives attention to those who are disadvantaged and vulnerable, and he places obligations to God above obligations owed the government when he is asked about paying taxes. How believers relate to the government is to be determined first by what God expects of them. It is hard to imagine that this does not include having governments move toward conforming their social and economic policies to God's will. This becomes the inescapable conclusion when we remember the way the mission of Jesus is described in the Magnificat:

> He has brought down the powerful from their thrones,
>   and lifted up the lowly:
> he has filled the hungry with good things,
>   and sent the rich away empty. (Luke 1:52–53)

This kingdom of Jesus is not something just made in heaven—it is what God wants for the way governments are structured in this world. We saw a bit of what that would look like when Jesus told his fellow diners that the people they should invite to their feasts are those who cannot return the invitation. This was more than telling them to help poor people. This was a rejection of the way the patronage system worked. Jesus calls those privileged and wealthy people at the banquet to reject a central part of the economic and social system of the day. That would mean accepting costly financial disadvantages. The mission of Jesus and his church includes seeking more just and merciful economic systems, including establishing policies and laws that expect the wealthy people to contribute more and that give advantages to those who are lower on the social and economic scale.

Jesus did not lobby to change tax laws, but that is no excuse for the church to avoid the work of shaping governmental social and economic policy. For example, Jesus did not work to enact laws that prohibit human trafficking, but most of us would say the church should support laws that do. We have to remember that the political system was not one that allowed people in Jesus's social class to influence government policy. The political system of the Roman Empire frowned on any dissent from the artisan class. People could not turn to democratic institutions for help. Our political environment is very different. As citizens, we have the right, even the obligation, to influence public policy. If we exercise that right as Christian citizens, we must move the government to create policies that extend the mission of Jesus to stop suffering and end oppression. In Luke, that clearly includes constructing systems and laws that privilege the needs of those who are poor, including when that means sending the rich away empty.

A church that listens to Luke's message will be countercultural. When the church speaks in favor of laws that require the wealthy to relinquish some of their wealth so that government programs can better meet the needs of people who are struggling, it will face criticism and opposition. We should expect nothing less. Being a faithful witness to God's will has often brought opposition and even persecution. Luke's message demands that the church have these conversations within its walls. Perhaps one way to begin is with a practice known as Deliberative Dialogue.[1] This is a process in which people identify the values they see at stake in thinking about particular issues. With this starting point, a church can then think about weighing these values and discerning which values are Christian values and which are more cultural.

Living with the Power of Sin

Our study of Paul gave us an analysis of the world that is distressing. He acknowledges that the social and cultural systems that govern the world are controlled by Sin. Those systems do not always seek the best for all people and do not reflect the justice, mercy, and goodness of God. But he also says that Christians are freed from the control of the power of Sin. This freedom enables us to fight Sin in all its manifestations, including governmental policies that fail to provide for the needs of people who are disadvantaged and continue to favor the privileged. He also warns us that we are all tainted by self-interest. At the same time, we are strengthened by the Spirit to work toward God's will for the whole world that is enslaved by Sin. It is the church's job to engage the battle against Sin in what it teaches about personal morality and what it teaches about social and economic values and justice.

As we try to discern God's will, our judgment will also be tainted by self-interest. Sin within us cannot be completely rooted out. This suggests that churches who are actively trying to do the will of God will listen to other Christians who think other parts of God's will are being harmed by what they advocate. This humility need not, however, keep the church from pressing toward its best understanding of the will of God. These Romans texts also remind us that no political party or platform is free of self-interest. The church can stand apart from partisan politics by focusing on issues and pointing to ways all political parties fall short of God's will.

Before we leave Romans, we should notice at least one thing about Romans 13. This is a difficult chapter that instructs the church in Rome that they should pay their taxes to the government. We noted at the beginning of this study that some claim the Bible does not suggest that governments should demand justice for their people. D. C. Innes cited Romans 13 as evidence for this view, saying that when Paul discusses the function of government he does not mention doing good. But that is not quite correct. If we read Romans 13 carefully we will notice that Paul says the authorities are "servants of God for your good" (v. 4). This suggests that he thinks governing authorities should be working for the good of the people. He does not say what this includes, but he does say that the government should be working for the good of its people.

We saw in our study of Philippians 2 that Paul makes the self-giving love of Christ the pattern for how believers should relate to one another. Paul calls the Philippians to put the needs of others ahead of their own good. That is a radical and countercultural demand in both the first century and today. We also saw that the liturgy Paul quotes has God make Christ the ruler of the cosmos in the present. Since Christ is Lord now, all things in the world should be subject to him, not just things in the church. While Christ has begun to reign, it is clear that the world is not yet fully subject to him. But the church should be the place where Christ's reign is acknowledged and where its members are subject to his lordship. If we live out our subjection to Christ in all areas of our lives, it will mean that we work to bring more of the world into subjection to his will. Since he is already the God-appointed Lord of the whole world, the church will work to bring all of creation into conformity with his will. That will include the kinds of policies and laws that our governments formulate and enforce. Speaking in favor of self-giving love may set the church at odds with the values that most people live by and may make us seem rather naïve. But the blessings that come to Christians when their churches live out self-giving love can be a demonstration of the value of this way of living.

Responsible to God

Finally, we saw that Revelation shows us that God holds governments and their leaders responsible for how they wield power. Rome is condemned not just for persecuting Christians, but also for its violence and its economic system. God condemns Rome for policies that help those who are wealthy maintain their wealth and position. Again we see that the goal of God's action is to have the world's governments conformed to God's will: "The kingdom of this world has become the kingdom of our Lord and of his Christ" (Rev 11:5).

All that we have seen indicates that God expects governments to have policies, laws, and institutions that reflect who God is. They are to embody and promote the justice, mercy, and goodness of God. God expects government policies and institutions to protect the people who are vulnerable and poor. But more than that, God wants governments to give advantages to those who need help, because such policies and laws reflect God's mercy and goodness. God expects governments to provide for the needs of people who are vulnerable (widows and orphans are singled out in what we saw), including making sure that laws do not allow their exploitation.

Practicing Self-Giving Love

Perhaps the most demanding expectation we have seen is that Christians are to make the self-giving love of Christ the guide for how they treat all people. As Paul talks about this expectation, he says that it means placing the good of others above our own. This text and nearly all the texts we have looked at reject the individualistic cultural outlook that dominates western, and especially American, culture. We say each person should look out for his or her own good. We encourage people to pull themselves up by their own bootstraps. But if the self-giving love of Christ calls us to work not for our own good but for the good of others, this is to be the guide for public policy as much as it is for personal life.

Does this mean that God favors "big government"? Well, it depends. Remember that the biblical message generally condemns nations for violence against those governed and against other nations. This can suggest that God favors reducing the amount nations spend on weapons of war. Perhaps it would mean spending less on mass incarceration, especially of ethnic minorities. This would require prisons to become more about reform, and less about punishment. It would also demand significant social and economic changes that give hope before people turn to crime. These examples suggest that in some instances God's will could call for less government spending and in some instances more.

Working to have God's will shape policies, laws, and institutions does not mean that the government should require religious activities in schools and government offices and institutions. Governmental displays of religious signs and worship have never been among the central things God wants. Remember that the temple in Jerusalem offered prayers and sacrifices right up to the day the nation fell. Then as now, God was more concerned about laws that protect people who are poor and vulnerable (as the Hebrew prophets remind us). Working for a world that is governed by God's will includes being sure there is room for people to reject God. If the church tries to impose its will on people's religious lives, that would be another example of letting self-interest reign. The church's purpose in working for God's will is not about gaining power to dictate what people believe or how they should be religious. This work is about freeing all of God's children to live into the fullness of the life God has given them. In America, the separation of church and state was designed to make sure that people would not be required to support or obey a church. It was not intended to remove religious beliefs or churches from debates about our laws, institutions, and policies.

Our Christian faith demands that we work for and support programs that make our social, political, and economic systems more just and more merciful. Every policy that protects wealthy people and leaves unmet the needs of people who are poor and vulnerable violates the justice and mercy of God. Since the church stands as the institution that submits to the lordship of Christ, it must proclaim that the values it derives from who we know God to be in Christ are the values the whole world should live by because Christ is Lord of the whole cosmos. To do less is to fail to live up to our identity. To advocate for the justice, goodness, and mercy of God in all the structures of our government's laws and policies is an important way of living up to our identity as God's church.

How churches go about working for what God wants for the world will differ. Many can have programs that help people who have needs. Many already support programs such as food banks and housing shelters. Others adopt schools in economically depressed areas or have ways to help meet clothing needs of people who cannot afford what they need. Still others can offer legal or financial services to people who need them. It is vital for the church to be involved in these kinds of programs, which are a clear witness to the love God has for all people. But they are not enough.

Our study shows that God would have people who live in a democracy work to change laws, systems, and institutions that give advantages to the privileged and hold back those who have fewer resources and less power. Since God expects governments to reflect God's justice and mercy, God expects those who can vote to allow those values to determine who and what they vote for. The church can help its members and the broader society discern which positions reflect what God wants. Churches can become places of civil discourse on such questions. Opening our doors to debates about policy can help us live out our mission to the world. We can call for conversations that lift up God's expectations for government and public policy. What better place could there be for such deliberation?

Jeremiah called the people of Judah who were exiled to Babylon to "seek the welfare of the city" they were now required to live in. The church today also is called to seek the good of its city and nation by working to bring its laws and social, political, and economic systems closer to the will of God. I hope this study will help you have conversations with others about our current governmental policies and institutional systems. Discuss how or whether they bring more justice and extend God's mercy, especially to support people who are socially and economically disadvantaged.

Such conversations can be challenging, but the biblical witness we have explored calls people of faith to talk and to act, seeking governments and public policies that mirror what God wants for all people.

Questions for Discussion

1. What, if anything, has most surprised you about the Bible's expectations for governments? Why do you think we have not heard about these expectations as often as we hear about a theme such as personal salvation?

2. How do you think it would change the discussion about public policy inside the church if we always made the love, mercy, and justice of God the criteria for deciding which position Christians should take?

3. As Christians of differing political leanings discuss policies, how would regularly reminding each other of the taint of self-interest change our discussion? In what ways does self-interest result in partisanship?

4. Often, mutual confession of sin can be a powerful starting point for meaningful discussion. How might starting our conversations about politics sound different if we began with the confession that we have not believed that following Christ's example means putting the good of others ahead of our own good?

5. How might we begin to take more seriously the demand to follow Christ's example of privileging the needs of others? How might we begin to follow

that example in church? At work? In our discussions of social and economic issues and policies? In our discussions of immigration policies?

6. What could your own church or faith community do to address the issues of justice in your own community or in the wider world? Make a list of such issues and plan how you will discuss and address them.

Notes

Introduction: Is It That Bad or Is It Politics As Usual?

1. Richard C. Chewing, "Editor's Perspective," in *Biblical Principles and Public Policy: The Practice*, Christians in the Marketplace Series, ed. Richard C. Chewing (Colorado Springs: Navpress, 1991), 75–78.

2. D. C. Innes, "On the Role of Government," in *Left, Right & Christian: Evangelical Faith in Politics* (Boise, ID: Elevate Faith, 2016), 58–64.

Chapter 4
Acts: The Earliest Church and Economic Systems

1. Richard Weiss, "The Prophets and Illusory Views of Reality," at Lexington Theological Seminary TEACH-IN: Now What? Empowering the Church in the New Political Age, January 20, 2017.

Chapter 11
Being a Faithful Church in Today's World

1. See more details about Deliberative Dialogue at the Kettering Foundation website, https://www.kettering.org. For a discussion of how this might work in a church, see Leah D. Schade, *Preaching in the Purple Zone: Ministry in the Red-Blue Divide* (Lanham, MD: Rowman & Littlefield, 2019).